Science
Workbook

1

Deborah Roberts
Terry Hudson

Alan Haigh
Geraldine Shaw

Language consultants:
John McMahon
Liz McMahon

OXFORD

Great Clarendon Street, Oxford, OX2 6DP, United Kingdom

Oxford University Press is a department of the University of Oxford. It furthers the University's objective of excellence in research, scholarship, and education by publishing worldwide. Oxford is a registered trade mark of Oxford University Press in the UK and in certain other countries.

© Deborah Roberts, Terry Hudson 2021

The moral rights of the authors have been asserted.

First published in 2016

All rights reserved. No part of this publication may be reproduced, stored in a retrieval system, or transmitted, in any form or by any means, without the prior permission in writing of Oxford University Press, or as expressly permitted by law, by licence or under terms agreed with the appropriate reprographics rights organization. Enquiries concerning reproduction outside the scope of the above should be sent to the Rights Department, Oxford University Press, at the address above.

You must not circulate this work in any other form and you must impose this same condition on any acquirer.

British Library Cataloguing in Publication Data

Data available

ISBN 978-1-382006606

9 10

Paper used in the production of this book is a natural, recyclable product made from wood grown in sustainable forests. The manufacturing process conforms to the environmental regulations of the country of origin.

Printed in China by Golden Cup

Acknowledgements

The publisher and authors would like to thank the following for permission to use photographs and other copyright material:

Cover: Artwork by Blindsalida. **Photos: p13:** absolute-india/Shutterstock; **p27(l):** Khoroshunova Olga/Shutterstock; **p27(r):** hagit berkovich/Shutterstock; **p45(tl):** Babimu/Fotolia; **p45(tm):** Elena Elisseeva/Shutterstock; **p45(tr):** Tesgro Tessieri/Fotolia; **p45(ml):** Shutterstock; **p45(m):** Karol Kozłowski/Fotolia; **p45(mr):** Elenathewise/Fotolia; **p45(bl):** Shutterstock; **p45(bm):** Shutterstock; **p45(br):** Elnur/Shutterstock; **p46(a):** Fotos593/Shutterstock; **p46(b):** Dan Kosmayer/Shutterstock; **p46(c):** Fotofermer/Shutterstock; **p46(d):** Elnur/Shutterstock; **p46(e):** Antonova Ganna/Shutterstock; **p51(tl):** © Michelle Lowry; **p51(tr):** Africa Studio/Shutterstock; **p55:** Shutterstock; **p78(t):** apple2499/Shutterstock; **p105(b):** Aleksandr Simonov/Shutterstock; **p105(b):** Pavelk/Shutterstock; **p105(b):** Edw/Shutterstock.

Artwork by Six Red Marbles and Q2A Media Services Pvt. Ltd.

Every effort has been made to contact copyright holders of material reproduced in this book. Any omissions will be rectified in subsequent printings if notice is given to the publisher.

Contents

How to Use this Book	5
Support for Teachers and Parents	6

1 Exploring Animals — 12

Introduction	13
Sorting animals	14
The vertebrate groups	16
What eats what?	18
Sorting some unusual animals	20
Same but different	22
Our body	24
Our senses: seeing, hearing	26
Our senses: tasting, smelling, touching	28
What I have learned about exploring animals	30

2 What is it Made of? — 32

Introduction	33
Different materials	34
What do materials look and feel like?	36
What can materials do?	38
What else can materials do?	40
Metals	42
Metals and non-metals	44
Useful materials	46
Sorting materials into groups	48
What I have learned about materials	50

3 Pushes and Pulls — 52

Introduction	53
Stopping and starting	54
Look at things moving in wind	56
Look at things moving in water and wind	58
Explore how things move (pushes and pulls)	60
Fast and slow-moving objects	62
Exploring the movement of toys	64
What I have learned about pushes and pulls	66

4 Making Sounds — 68

Introduction	69
Talking and listening	70
Making sounds	72
Quiet and loud sounds	74
Sounds and moving about	76
Sounds around us	78
How we hear sounds	80
What I have learned about making sounds	82

5 Plants and the Seasons **84**

Introduction 85
Parts of a plant 86
Looking at wild and
　garden plants 88
Weather 90
The seasons 92
Recording rainfall 94
Observing and measuring
　the wind 96
What I have learned about
　plants and the seasons 98

Quiz Yourself **100**

How to Use this Book

The Workbook for *Oxford International Primary Science* supports the Student Book that children are using in their science lessons for this year.

The Student Book includes some pair, group and whole-class activities, hands-on tasks and write-in tasks to test students' understanding and help them learn. It is important to extend these tasks. This Workbook enables students to build on what they have learned in the Student Book to develop a secure understanding of scientific concepts.

Encouraging students to think about and apply their growing skills and knowledge helps them consolidate their understanding and work scientifically. This helps with confidence. Students also have opportunities to see that science is relevant all around them – both inside and outside the classroom.

Students may find it useful to complete an investigation planning form. This sets out all the stages of the investigation. A proforma is provided in the Teacher's Guide. Find out more at:

www.oxfordprimary.com/international-science

Structure of the book

This Workbook is divided into five units plus a Support for Teachers and Parents section and a Quiz:

Support for Teachers and Parents
Unit 1 Exploring Animals
Unit 2 What is it Made of?
Unit 3 Pushes and Pulls
Unit 4 Making Sounds
Unit 5 Plants and Seasons
Quiz Yourself

What you will find in each unit

There are four types of lessons:

Key words and introduction lessons encourage students to read, spell and use the scientific vocabulary in the unit.

Activities build on the work in the Student Book. These help with developing language skills, developing scientific enquiry skills, applying mathematical knowledge and securing understanding rather than just recall. The Support for Teachers and Parents notes on pages 6–11 give you advice on how to help students with each activity.

What I have learned encourages students to talk about what they have learned, reflect on what went well and revisit any areas they need to check. This encourages a growth mindset.

Investigate like a scientist enables students to apply what they have learned in practical contexts.

What you will find in the lessons

Icons show the nature of each task:

Discuss: Students are encouraged to discuss and communicate scientific ideas and approaches. They can work in pairs or small groups for discussion tasks.

Investigate: Students are encouraged to plan, ask questions and record results for each investigation. They are asked to observe closely, make predictions and compare their results with others. Sometimes you will use different equipment, which is available in school. You may also ask students to carry out a test in a different way, to make sure they are safe.

Language support: This icon highlights activities that provide language support through writing frames or word banks. Students are encouraged to write, read and record short answers.

Hints and tips: Students are encouraged to think about tips to make investigations safer or more effective.

Stretch zone: Students are encouraged to extend their understanding.

Mindful moments: Students are encouraged to think about and reflect on what they have learned. This supports students' well-being.

What went well: Students are encouraged to talk about what went well in each module to secure their understanding.

Student Book

Throughout the Workbook, you will find links to the Student Book. Students can refer to information in the Student Book to help them complete activities.

Teacher's Guide

The Teacher's Guide that accompanies this book provides lesson notes and answers for each page.

Support for Teachers and Parents

1 Exploring Animals

What students will learn
This unit helps students to understand more about themselves and the variety of common animals. Students will:
- identify examples of animals that are herbivores, omnivores and carnivores
- learn that all living things depend on each other
- learn to group animals into vertebrates and invertebrates, and the five classes: fish, amphibians, reptiles, birds and mammals
- learn the main parts of animals and use observation skills to compare and contrast them
- learn the basic parts of the human body and how each is associated with each sense.

Key words
amphibian, bird, carnivore, fish, herbivore, mammal, omnivore, reptile, senses

Scientific enquiry skills
This unit helps students to develop and practise the following scientific enquiry skills.

Scientific enquiry skill	Page
Observe	13, 14, 16, 17, 23, 25, 26
Compare	13, 15, 16, 17, 18, 19, 20
Notice patterns	14, 15, 18, 27
Record	12, 14, 18, 19, 22, 24, 26, 29
Carry out tests	19, 28, 29
Group/classify	14, 15, 16, 17, 18, 20
Use secondary sources	19, 20, 24, 27

Ways to help
- Place key words on a word wall. Add to them during the unit.
- Measure objects using students' hands and then a ruler.
- Encourage students to look around them and ask questions about what they see.
- Collect pictures of different animals for students to observe and sort.

Helping with activities
The following guidance gives you advice on how to help students with each activity.

Sorting groups
Talk about the objects in the picture. Ask students how the objects are different and which ones are similar. Discuss the possible groupings students could use.

Find the vertebrates
Help students to identify the animals with bone inside their bodies – vertebrates. The others are invertebrates.

Group the animals
You can help students by explaining that at each stage of the key a decision is made and this determines which branch of the key to follow.

Types of vertebrates
Encourage students to look very carefully at the animals in the pictures. Ask them about the various features they can see and then ask them to identify each animal.

What eats what?
Help students by pointing out that they should observe the animals in the picture carefully. Remind them about the differences between the vertebrate classes.

What do pets eat?
Once students have done their survey of pets, ask them to record their findings in the table. They then decide whether each pet is a carnivore, herbivore or omnivore.

Unusual vertebrates
Encourage students to look at the main features used to classify the vertebrate groups and then apply these to each animal.

Living on an icy planet
Help students by pointing out that no matter how unusual the surroundings, they can apply the same rules as they apply to animals in their region.

Faces
Encourage students to carry out the tasks a few times for each part, as this repetition will help to consolidate learning.

Drawing faces
Help students by talking to them about the main features of the face – eyes, mouth and nose in particular.

Challenge: body parts
Encourage students to talk about the parts of the body before they start to label their body outline. Remind them to tick each word as they draw the outline of their hand.

Body parts game
Make a set of body part cards for each group of students. You can use pieces of card or sticky notes.

Name the senses
Help students by pointing out the word box at the top. Explain it is there to help them with the spelling. Read through the words with them.

Animal senses
Encourage students to use their observation skills to study the animals carefully. Talk to them about the different features linked to senses.

Sense of smell
Encourage students to sit very quietly and still for the activity. After the activity ask them to talk about any pattern they saw in the raised hands.

Sense trail
Help students to look for the various objects and make sure you have placed some around the room prior to the activity. They are warned not to taste anything without your permission so you may wish to have some safe and available foods for them to try.

What I have learned about exploring animals
Help students to reflect on each statement and to decide how well they know this aspect of the unit.

Investigate like a scientist: Make a model head
Remind students to think about their investigations and tests as they are doing them and to change their plans and ideas if things are not working.

2 What is it Made of?

What students will learn
This unit helps students to understand more about materials and their properties. Students will:
- distinguish between an object and the material from which it is made
- identify and name a variety of everyday materials, including wood, plastic, glass, metal, water and rock
- describe the simple physical properties of a variety of everyday materials
- compare and group together a variety of everyday materials on the basis of their simple physical properties.

Key words
fabric, glass, material, metal, paper, plastic, rock, water, wood

Scientific enquiry skills
This unit helps students to develop and practise the following scientific enquiry skills.

Scientific enquiry skill	Page
Observe	34, 35, 36, 38, 39, 40, 41, 42, 44, 46, 47
Compare	36, 38, 39, 40, 41, 42, 45, 46, 49
Notice patterns	40, 41
Record	32, 35, 36, 40, 42, 43, 44, 47
Carry out tests	37, 38, 39, 40, 46, 49
Group/classify	33, 35, 36, 45, 47, 48, 49

Ways to help
- Encourage students to practise spelling and using key words.
- Set out a range of objects made from different materials.
- Remind students that they need to look at materials but also touch them.
- Ask students questions about the materials they use.
- Keep linking materials to their properties.
- Ask students why objects are made from certain materials.
- Play games by asking students to suggest materials that would be useless for certain jobs.
- Encourage students to test materials by feeling and stretching them.
- Allow students time to consider the 'stretch' activities, as these are more demanding.

Helping with activities
The following guidance gives you advice on how to help students with each activity.

I spy
Take the first turn in the game so you can demonstrate how it works. Stress the first letter of the word of the object.

Different materials game
Set out some examples of each material in an easy to find place. Leave some more hidden.

Label properties
You can pre-make the labelled sticky notes if students find the writing too difficult at this stage.

Hard and soft materials
Make sure the modelling clay is soft and easy to shape at the start as this will make a good contrast with the very hard clay after drying.

Which material is best for making a raincoat?
Before students start, discuss what they already know and remember about the different materials. This will help in their predictions.

Make a waterproof cover
Make sure students select an object that will not be damaged if it becomes wet. Have a large bucket of water available so they can test their designs.

Which materials can stretch?
Explain the table and stress that the right-hand column shows the length of the material after it has been stretched.

Floating and sinking
Make sure you have some heavy and light wooden objects in the room for students. Have a large bowl of water or a sink available. Students can find their own round objects for the second test.

Is metal best?
Set out a range of metal objects such as tools, ornaments, picture frames, containers, nails and screws so students can find a reasonable range of examples.

Useful metal objects
Encourage students to use their imagination when imagining a material other than a metal being used for the hammer.

Metal or non-metal?
Remind students that metals can be stretched, twisted and bent without breaking. Non-metals often break.

Properties of metals and non-metals
Remind students to use the words in the word box to help them and tell them that they can use some of the words more than once.

Making a model bridge and testing it
Encourage students to fold the card into different shapes and to try using more than one layer of card.

More useful metal objects
Show some objects made from aluminium, copper, gold, silver and steel. Allow students to discuss the one object they have chosen to talk about and encourage them to link the object, the material and its use.

Soft or hard?
Explain how to use the sorting hoops and place one or two objects in as a demonstration first.

Making music
Collect a range of metal and non-metal objects for students to test. Make sure the metal objects are thin and preferably hollow.

What I have learned about materials
Help students to reflect on each statement and to decide how well they know this aspect of this unit.

Investigate like a scientist: Testing designs
Remind students to think about their investigations and tests as they are doing them and to change their plans and ideas if things are not working.

3 Pushes and Pulls

What students will learn
This unit helps students to understand more about the forces of push and pull. Students will:
- explore pushes and pulls
- understand that pushes and pulls are forces
- learn what makes things speed up, slow down or change direction.

Key words
fast, move, pull, push, slow, stop

Scientific enquiry skills
This unit helps students to develop and practise the following scientific enquiry skills.

Scientific enquiry skill	Page
Observe	52, 53, 54, 56, 57, 58, 60
Compare	54, 58, 59, 61, 62, 63, 64, 65
Notice patterns	58, 59, 63
Record	53, 55, 56, 60, 61, 62, 63, 64
Carry out tests	52, 53, 55, 58, 59, 65
Group/classify	60, 62
Use secondary sources	62, 64

Ways to help
- Write the key words onto cards and place them onto a wall.
- Encourage students to say the word 'push' or 'pull' as they make things move.
- Show students everyday examples of pushes and pulls.
- Help students to use pushes and pulls.
- Explain that bigger pushes and pulls have a bigger effect on objects.
- Use examples of pushes and pulls that students will find relevant, e.g. sports.

- Let students move as many objects as possible and see that they change direction and speed when pushes and pulls are used.
- Encourage students to predict what effect pushes and pulls will have before they try them.
- Allow students to talk to each other about pushes and pulls to share ideas.

Helping with activities

The following guidance gives you advice on how to help students with each activity.

Using your body
Encourage students to kick the ball gently around the room but to also drag the ball back with their feet so they are using pushes and pulls.

Toy car
Show students how to start the toy car and ask them to suggest how it can be stopped before you let them work in their pairs or small groups.

Looking at flags
If there are no examples of flags in your area, you can show film from YouTube so that students see many examples.

Making bunting
Point out to students that they are also using pushes and pulls to make the bunting and to hang it up.

Making a sailing boat
Demonstrate making the boat to students and select large bottle tops or lids so they float and are stable in the water.

Making boats move
Show students the baster and show how the bulb is squeezed to make air come out of the end. Point out that this is a push force.

More pushes and pulls
Encourage students to move carefully around the room to search for pushes and pulls. Leave some toys and sports equipment out so they can try these.

Examples of pushing and pulling
Encourage students to use their observation skills and then to share their experiences of pulling hard.

Fast and slow
Help students to understand that they should speak slowly or quickly by saying some of the words you use to introduce the task very slowly and some very quickly.

Swing
Consider taking students out to a nearby park to investigate actual swings.

Making a toy car move
Collect different types of model cars so students can investigate small and large ones.

Design and build a moving vehicle
Talk to students about their designs before they start so they can think through what they are going to do and make sure they have all of the equipment they need.

What I have learned about pushes and pulls
Help students to reflect on each statement and to decide how well they know this aspect of this unit.

Investigate like a scientist: Playing with pushes and pulls
Demonstrate the task by doing the first example yourself – turn the paper over and if it says 'push', then push the ball.

4 Making Sounds

What students will learn
This unit helps students to understand more about sound and how to make and measure sounds. Students will:
- name some of the sources of sounds
- find out what happens to sounds when we move about
- understand that our ears hear sounds.

Key words
loud, quiet, sound, voice

Scientific enquiry skills
This unit helps students to develop and practise the following scientific enquiry skills.

Scientific enquiry skill	Page
Observe	71, 75, 76, 77, 79
Compare	68, 70, 71, 72, 74, 75, 76, 78, 80, 81, 83
Notice patterns	70, 72, 75, 76, 78
Record	68, 69, 70, 71, 74, 75, 79, 80
Carry out tests	70, 72, 75, 76, 77, 78, 80
Group/classify	74, 76
Use secondary sources	72, 74, 75, 78, 80, 81

Ways to help
- Read out all of the key words and ask students to say which ones they have heard of before.

- Practise the key words by gently tapping a desk and have students say 'quiet'.
- Bang the desk and have students say 'loud'.
- Collect examples of musical instruments to let students try.
- Have periods of silence in the room so students can hear sounds from outside.
- Download songs that students can sing along to.
- Check if anyone is having music lessons and ask them to share their ideas.
- Encourage students to talk about the different sounds they hear.
- Be aware that some students may have hearing impairments, and be sensitive to this.

Helping with activities

The following guidance gives you advice on how to help students with each activity.

Your voice
After students have practised making the sounds with their voices, ask for some volunteers to come out and show the class.

Sing!
Play some recorded music that demonstrates harmonies to help students realise how voices can combine by singing slightly different notes.

Clap your hands
Spread the class out for this activity as otherwise the clapping can become confusing. Try to use a larger hall or an outside space. If this is not possible, get the pairs to take it in turn.

Make music using your lips
Ensure that students hold the tracing paper close to the comb so they get maximum vibrations, otherwise the sounds will not be clear or loud enough.

Listen carefully
Point out that people hear things slightly differently so not to worry if someone can hear a sound while they can't. Monitor this, as you may detect some hearing problems that you can report.

Measuring sounds in school
Survey the school first so you can identify areas where there will be fairly loud noises – such as near delivery bays or machinery – and some quiet areas like learning centres or medical rooms.

Sounds near and far
This is another activity that works best in a large space. Take students outside if possible so they can move many metres apart.

Surprise!
Check that there are no reflective surfaces in front of the student at the front otherwise they will be able to watch the approaching students.

Moving quietly
You could film students on a digital camera or smartphone and play it back so they can listen to themselves.

Useful loud noises
If you do not hear sirens very often near the school, then download some sounds or film from the internet to play to the class.

Hearing
Show some pictures of animals with very large ears to act as a clue that the ears trap sound waves and funnel them into the ear.

Measuring sounds in decibels
Show students some ear protectors and stress that anyone working near loud noises should wear them. Remind them that music through earphones can be loud enough to damage hearing.

What I have learned about making sounds
Help students to reflect on each statement and to decide how well they know this aspect of this unit.

Investigate like a scientist: Comparing different sounds
Find a large open space and make sure it is safe with no trip hazards.

5 Plants and the Seasons

What students will learn

This unit helps students to understand more about the structure of plants and how the weather and the seasons are linked. Students will:

- identify and name a variety of common wild and garden plants, including deciduous and evergreen trees
- identify and describe the basic structure of a variety of common flowering plants, including trees
- observe changes across the four seasons
- observe and describe weather associated with the seasons and how day length varies.

Key words
flower, leaf, plant, roots, season, stem, trunk, wild

Scientific enquiry skills

This unit helps students to develop and practise the following scientific enquiry skills.

Scientific enquiry skill	Page
Observe	84, 86, 87, 89, 91, 93, 94
Compare	85, 87, 89, 91, 92, 93, 97, 99
Notice patterns	90, 92, 93, 95, 96
Record	84, 86, 87, 90, 91, 93, 95
Carry out tests	93, 95, 96
Group/classify	84, 88, 89, 92
Use secondary sources	87, 90, 93, 95, 96, 97

Ways to help

- Encourage students to practise spelling and using the key words.
- Obtain a range of plants to display in the room.
- Identify places to take students to observe plants.
- Ask students questions about the plants they have seen before.
- Encourage students to practise drawing and labelling plants.
- Create a nature table or wall display for students to collect plant materials.
- Keep a log of the weather during and after the unit.
- Make large displays of the weather symbols and place the most appropriate one at the front of the classroom every day.
- Record weather forecasts for students to watch.
- Cut out weather reports and data from newspapers and keep a scrapbook.

Helping with activities

The following guidance gives you advice on how to help students with each activity.

Colour the parts of a plant
Remind students about the different parts of a flowering plant. You could have a large poster version visible in the room.

Make a plant display
Allow students to have access to the internet or print some pictures of plants for them. Arrange plant magazines and seed catalogues around the room.

Is it a tree or a shrub?
Remind students that a tree has a single main stem called a trunk. Shrubs have numerous, smaller stems.

Survey of flowering plants
Identify a safe place locally to take students to. Make sure there is a wide range of flowering plants, trees and shrubs.

Predicting the weather
Help students to learn the weather symbols by displaying large versions on a wall.

Types of weather
You could start by asking students about which type of weather disrupts things they like to do – such as playing sports or visiting local parks and beaches.

Which season is it?
Point out that different parts of the world can have different seasons. Within the tropical regions there are often two – rainy season and dry season.

Investigating seasons
Remind students that they need to use their observation skills and look carefully for clues about the seasons.

Observing the weather
Explain to students that weather means what is happening in the atmosphere at any one time, such as whether it is raining or sunny. Climate is what the weather is like over a long period. For example, a climate can be dry even if it rains sometimes.

Measuring rainfall
Show students how to empty the rain from their bottle after taking a reading and how to top up the water to the start of the gauge.

Windsocks
Prepare some card tubes to give to any students who may not be able to fold and fix the card to make their own.

Wind speeds
Explain that the Beaufort scale uses things that people can see happening to let them know the wind speed. Ask students what the wind speed would be if they can see small branches moving.

What I have learned about plants and the seasons
Help students to reflect on each statement and to decide how well they know this aspect of this unit.

Investigate like a scientist: Making a model plant
Show students the materials you have collected so they know what they can use before they start to plan their model.

1 Exploring Animals

Key words

1 Join the dots to make some important words for this unit.
   Each word is the name of a part of the body.

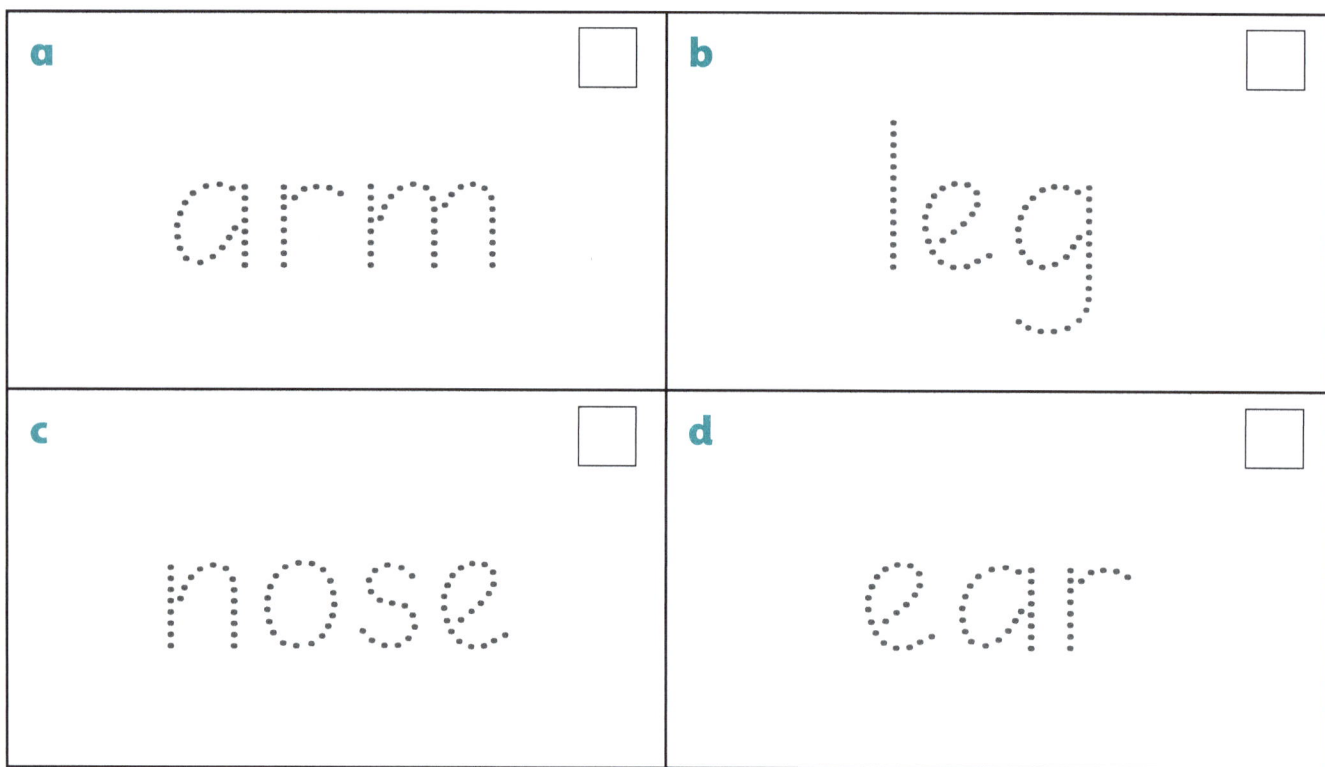

2 Tick ✓ the part of the body that you use to smell flowers.

3 Circle the part of the body that you use to listen to people talking.

Introduction

We are all different

1. Look at yourself in a mirror.

   Is your hair the same as the person in the photograph?

   Is your nose the same shape?

2. Draw a picture of yourself. Describe your eyes and mouth.

Sorting animals

Sorting groups

You have learned how we sort animals into groups (see pages 14–15 of your Student Book).

In this activity you will be sorting non-living objects.

1 Look at the objects in the picture.

Sort the objects into three groups.

Draw the objects in the circles. Use one circle for each group.

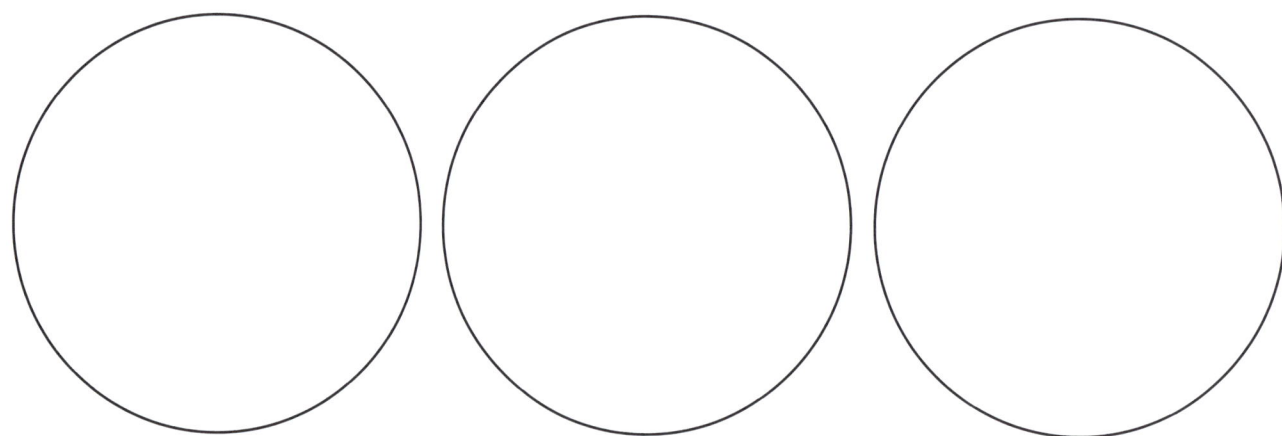

2 Think of a name for each group. Write the name at the top of the circle.

Find the vertebrates

 **Stretch zone**

1 A vertebrate is an _____ which has a _____.

> animal   backbone

2 An invertebrate is an _____ which has no _____.

3 A vet in a zoo has taken some X-rays of animals.

Help the vet to sort the animals into vertebrates and invertebrates.

Tick ✓ the vertebrates.

☐    ☐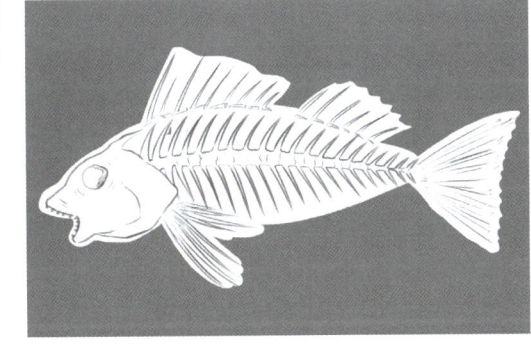

☐    ☐

The vertebrate groups

Group the animals

Look at the invertebrates below.

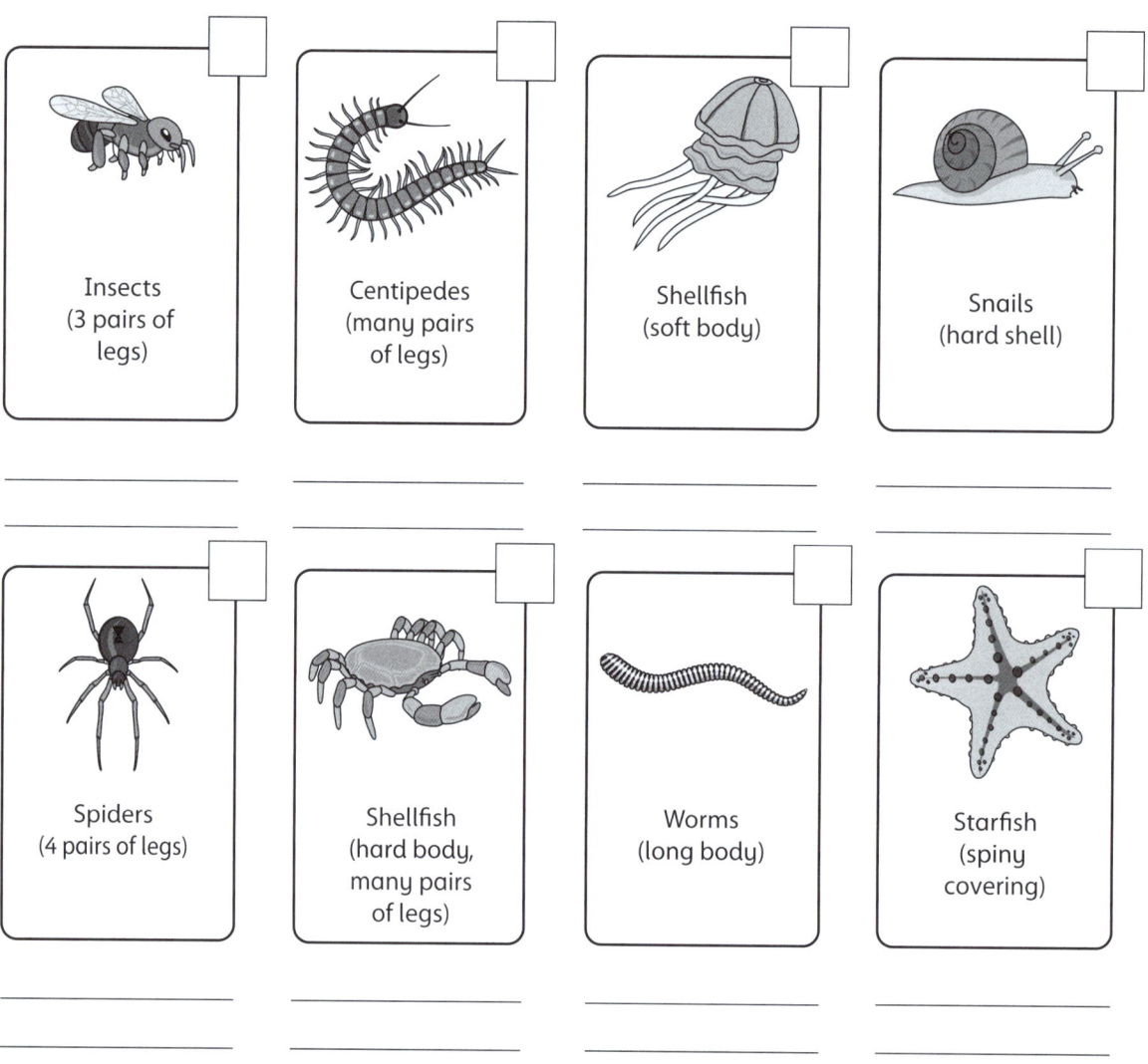

1. Tick ✓ the pictures of the invertebrates that have legs.
2. Count how many legs each animal has and write the number under the picture.
3. Write two ways that the spider is different to the snail.

   1 The spider has _____ .

   2 The snail has a _____ .

Types of vertebrates

1. Look at the pictures. Each shows a different type of vertebrate. Fill in the correct letters below.

   <u>c</u> is a mammal.

   ___ is an amphibian.

   ___ is a bird.

   ___ is a fish.

   ___ is a reptile.

2. Which type of animal would you like as a pet? _____

    Explain why.

    Think about the reasons for your answer.

What eats what?

What eats what?

1. Group the animals in the picture. Use pages 16–17 in your Student Book to help you. One has been done for you.

Examples of each type of animal found in the picture				
Amphibian	**Bird**	**Fish**	**Mammal**	**Reptile**
		angelfish		

2. Name two animals in the picture that might eat fish.

1 _____

2 _____

What do pets eat?

Use this activity to help you with your pet survey on page 19 of your Student Book.

1 Which pets do your classmates have? Find five people who have pets.
2 Ask each person what their pet eats.
3 Fill in the table below.
4 Decide if the pet is a carnivore, a herbivore or an omnivore.
5 Write this in your table. Write C for carnivore, H for herbivore or O for omnivore.

Type of pet	What it eats	Carnivore, herbivore or omnivore? (C, H or O)

6 What does each animal below eat?

deer   owl   bear

Find out if it is a carnivore, a herbivore or an omnivore.

1 Exploring Animals

Sorting some unusual animals

Unusual vertebrates

If you need help to answer these questions, ask an adult.

1 Why is a whale a mammal and not a fish?

   Write two reasons.

   1 _____

   2 _____

2 Why is a penguin a bird and not a fish?

   Write two reasons.

   1 _____

   2 _____

3 Why is a bat a mammal and not a bird?

   Write two reasons.

   1 _____

   2 _____

Stretch zone

Try to find a picture of a duck-billed platypus.

Which group of animals does this animal belong to?

Living on an icy planet

Imagine a large animal that lives on an icy planet:

- It lives in water.
- It has to keep warm, as the sea is very cold.
- It hunts fast-moving fish.
- It lays eggs.
- It cannot breathe under water.
- It has dry, scaly skin.
- It has a backbone.

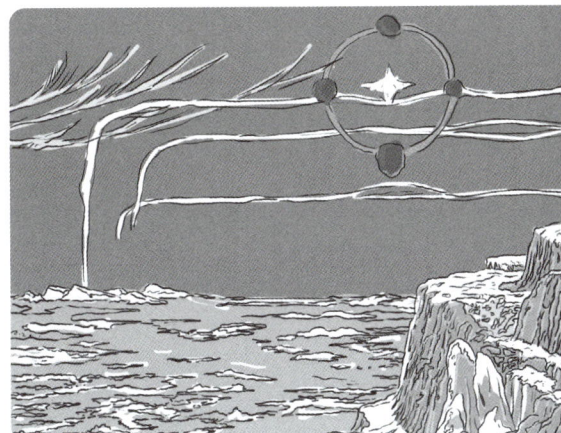

You have been asked to draw what the animal might look like.

Draw your animal in the box below.

 Stretch zone

Which animal class is the animal most likely to belong to?

Same but different

Faces

1 Draw a line to link each word with the correct part of the face. One has been done for you.

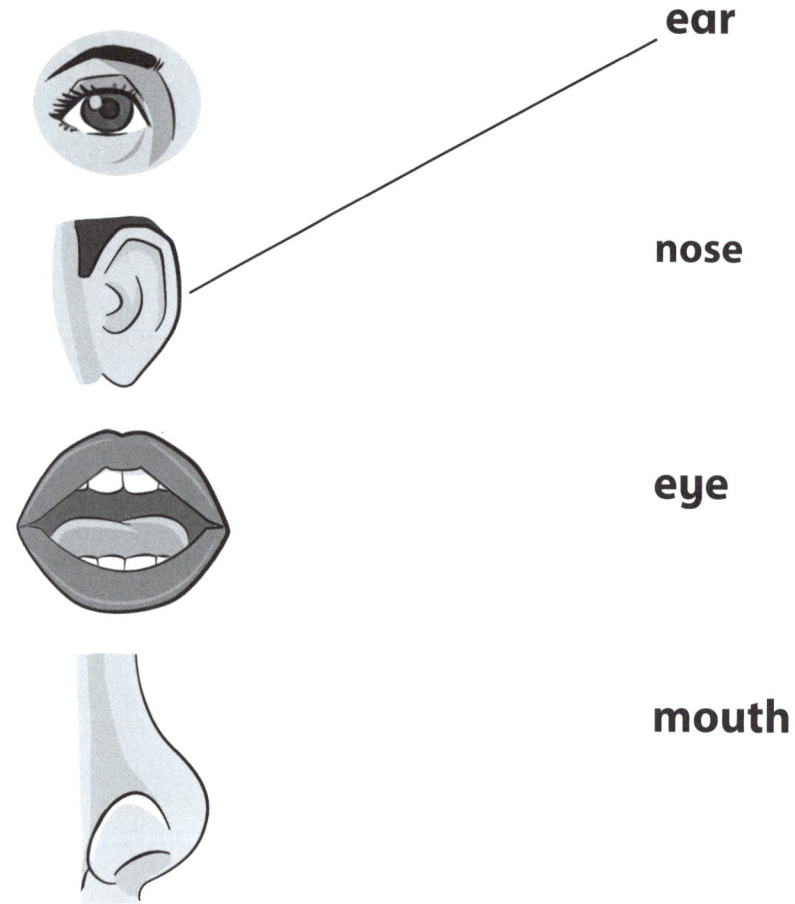

2 Point to each part of your face and say the word out loud.

3 Write in the missing words. Use the words from the word box. One has been done for you.

We are all _____.

We have some ___things___ that are the _____.

different   same   ~~things~~

Drawing faces

1 Draw three different faces on the heads. Show one person who is sad. Show one person who is happy. Show one person who is surprised.

2 Ask someone, 'Which person is happy? Which person is sad?'

3 Can they point to the person who is surprised?

Our body

Challenge: body parts

This activity is linked to the investigation on page 24 of your Student Book.

You will need: a piece of paper large enough to lie down on. You could stick lots of smaller pieces of paper together.

1 Draw around your partner's body.

2 Use the outline you have drawn to make a poster.
3 Colour in the outline and label the parts of the body.

Stretch zone

Draw around your own hand.

Tick ✓ each part you find.

fingers ☐   thumb ☐   fingernails ☐

wrist ☐   finger joints ☐

Now label these parts on your drawing.

Body parts game

 Play the body parts game.

a Your teacher will give you a set of cards with body part names on.

b Place the cards face down in front of you.

c Take a card and read the word out loud. Point to this part of the body. Ask your classmates if you are correct. Then it is the next person's turn.

Our senses: seeing, hearing

Name the senses

 Look at the pictures. Write the sense that matches each picture. Use the words in the box to help you.

| hearing |
| seeing |

Stretch zone

When you cross a busy road, which senses do you use to help you stay safe?

Animal senses

1 Look at the photographs and answer the questions.

   a Which animal do you think is good at hearing? Why?
   _____

   b Which animal do you think is good at seeing? Why?
   _____

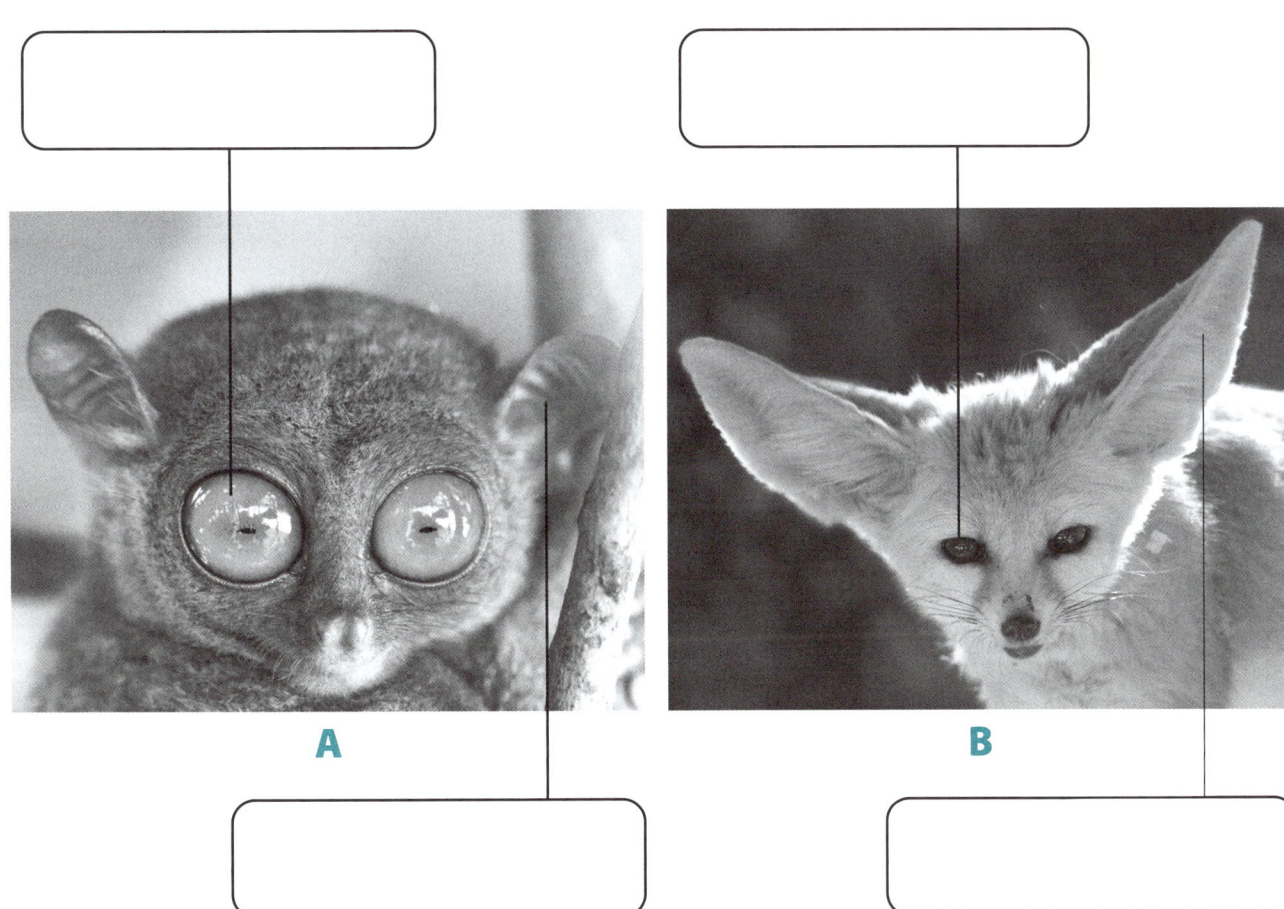

A   B

2 Now label each animal's face. Find the eyes and the ears.

Stretch zone

Cats have better hearing than humans. Cats can also move their ears to point in different directions. How do you think this helps them?

Our senses: tasting, smelling, touching

Sense of smell

1 Your teacher will check your sense of smell.

Sit quietly. When you can smell the perfume raise your hand.

Who smelled the perfume first? _____

Who smelled the perfume last? _____

2 Your teacher will test you with different smells.

Write down what you think the smells are.

Smell	What I think it is
1	
2	
3	
4	

Sense trail

1 Use your senses to find things.
2 Draw one example in each box.

Find something colourful.

Find something that makes a noise.

Find something with a nice smell.

Find something that feels smooth.

Find something that tastes good.

Warning! Do not taste anything without checking with an adult that it is safe.

What I have learned about exploring animals

1. Think about what you have learned.
2. Talk to a friend about something that went well in this unit.
3. Tick ✓ the boxes to rate yourself.

I can group animals into vertebrates and invertebrates.	That's easy. ☐ That's challenging. ☐	Pages 14–17
I can identify carnivores, herbivores and omnivores.	That's easy. ☐ That's challenging. ☐	Pages 18–19
I can sort unusual animals into groups.	That's easy. ☐ That's challenging. ☐	Pages 20–21
I know that we are all humans but we look different.	That's easy. ☐ That's challenging. ☐	Pages 22–23
I can point to my ears, eyes, nose, mouth, head and hair.	That's easy. ☐ That's challenging. ☐	Pages 24–25
I can name the five senses.	That's easy. ☐ That's challenging. ☐	Pages 26–27
I know each body part that is used for the five senses.	That's easy. ☐ That's challenging. ☐	Pages 28–29

If you want to know more or need to check, go back to the pages in your Student Book.

 **Investigate like a scientist**

Make a model head

You will need some modelling clay.

1 **Make a model head out of modelling clay.**

2 **Label the head to show: eyes, ears, nose and mouth.**

3 **Now make labels to link each part of the head with the following senses:**

> hear   see   smell   taste

You could also use fruit, such as a melon or an orange, and draw on features with a marker pen.

2 What is it Made of?

Key words

This is fabric.

We sometimes call this material.

Fabric is a type of material.

You will find out about other materials in this unit.

Join the dots to find the names of some of these materials.

a	b
wood	glass
c	**d**
metal	paper

Introduction

Materials

We make objects from materials.

Here are some of the materials you are going to explore in this unit.

glass   metal
paper   plastic
wood

1 Work with a partner.

   Point to each word in the word cloud and say it out loud.

   Talk about each of these materials.

2 Draw a line to match each word to a picture.

3 Write one more object that is made from each of the different materials.

   glass: _____   metal: _____

   paper: _____   plastic: _____

   wood: _____

Different materials

I spy

Play a game of 'I spy'.

The picture shows you how to play.

a Take turns to look for objects that are soft and hard.

b Choose one object but do not tell anyone what you have chosen.

c Everyone else takes turns to guess the object you have chosen.

Different materials game

1 Play this game with a partner.

   a You have 10 minutes to find objects made of different materials.

   b Who can find the most in 10 minutes?

   c Here are some different materials to look for.

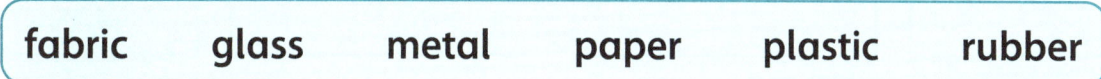

| fabric | glass | metal | paper | plastic | rubber |

2 Complete this table of results.

Name:		Name:	
Object	**Material**	**Object**	**Material**
Total:		Total:	

What do materials look and feel like?

Label properties

1. Read the properties in the boxes.
   With a partner, discuss what they mean.

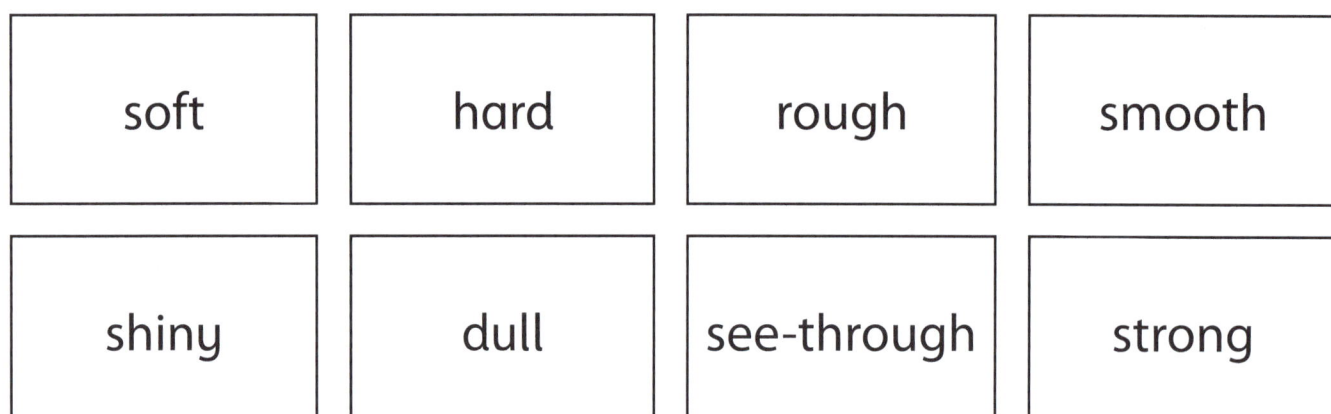

| soft | hard | rough | smooth |

| shiny | dull | see-through | strong |

2. Make a label for each property by writing each word on a sticky note.
3. Walk around the room and place each label on an object with that property.
4. Write your examples in the table. One has been done for you.

Name of the object	Property
table	hard

Hard and soft materials

Your teacher will give you a piece of modelling clay.

Look closely at the modelling clay.

1 Do you think it will be hard or soft?

   Circle your answer.

   hard   **soft**

2 Pick up the modelling clay. How does it feel?

   Circle your answer.

   hard   **soft**

3 Squeeze the modelling clay with your hands.

   Roll it into a sausage or snake shape. Does it feel softer now?

   Circle your answer.

   yes   **no**

4 Make your clay into a small pot.

   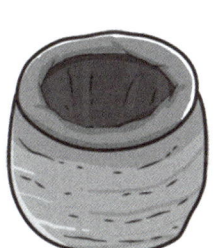

   Your teacher will tell you where to leave your pot to dry.

   When it is dry look closely at the pot.

   Do you think it will be hard or soft?

   Circle your answer.

   hard   **soft**

5 Pick up the pot. How does it feel?

   Circle your answer.

   hard   **soft**

   You can decorate your pot with paints or use glue to stick decorations on it.

What can materials do?

Which material is best for making a raincoat?

 This activity is linked to the investigation on page 38 of your Student Book.

Hint: What do you already know about the different materials?

You will test materials. You will find out which material makes the best waterproof raincoat.

Use these questions to help you plan your investigation.

I think that . . .

Which material do you guess (predict) will keep the cotton wool dry?

_____

Discuss with a partner why you think this.

Discuss what you will do . . .

How will you wrap your cotton wool?

Discuss what you are looking for . . .

Which material keeps the cotton wool the driest?

What did I find out?

Which material is the most waterproof? _____

Was your guess correct? Circle one word.

yes   **no**

 Stretch zone

 Talk about how you can make your investigation better.

Make a waterproof cover

1 Choose one object that is important to you. For example, a special toy, a book or a mobile phone.

My object is _____.

2 What is the best material to keep your object dry?

I will use _____.

3 Now design your waterproof cover.

What will you use to fix the cover together?

_____
_____

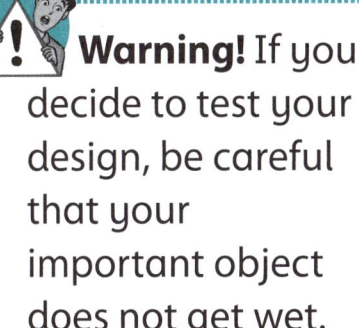

Warning! If you decide to test your design, be careful that your important object does not get wet.

Draw a picture of your design.

Stretch zone

Is a paper coat useful? How useful is a sponge umbrella?

What else can materials do?

Which materials can stretch?

This activity is linked to the investigation on page 40 of your Student Book.

A table is a quick way to record and organise results and observations. Scientists can then share these with other scientists.

1 Look at this table. Talk about what it shows.

Material tested	Length (cm)	Length (cm) after 20 g mass added
Plastic bag	20	25
Paper	20	20
Metal ruler	20	20
Elastic band	20	35

2 Find some different materials to test. Find out which material stretches the most.

3 Use the table to record your results. Remember to label your table.

Warning! Be careful when you stretch materials. Do not pull materials too strongly. They might snap and hurt you.

Floating and sinking

This is a raft made from wood. It floats.

You are going to investigate if all wooden objects float.

1 Look around the classroom for five wooden objects.

   Tick what you think will happen. This is your prediction.

   I think they will all float. ☐

   I think some will float and some will sink. ☐

   I think they will all sink. ☐

2 Check with your teacher that you can test each one.

3 Fill a large bowl with water or use a sink.

4 Test each wooden object to see if it floats or sinks.

Warning! Be careful because splashed water can make the floor slippery.

5 Record your results below.

Object	Did it float? (✓)	Did it sink? (✓)

6 Were your predictions correct? Circle the answer.   **Yes   No**

Stretch zone

Plan and carry out a test to see if all round objects sink. Tell a friend what you found out in your investigation.

Metals

Is metal best?

1 Look around the room. Find four objects made of metal.

2 Imagine if each object was made of glass, paper or rubber. Is it still useful?

Fill in the table.

Colour the boxes using traffic light colours.

☐ Green – the material is better than metal.

☐ Orange – the material is just as good as metal.

☐ Red – the material is not as good as metal.

An example has been done for you. Colour these boxes using the colours shown.

Metal object	If it was made of glass	If it was made of paper	If it was made of rubber
pan	orange	red	red

Useful metal objects

1. Think about the metal objects you use.

   Ask people, 'Which metal object do you use the most?'

2. Record your answers in the table.

Name of the person I asked	The metal object they use the most

Stretch zone

Look at the metal object in the picture. Imagine it is made of a different material. Draw your object. Try to imagine how it will work.

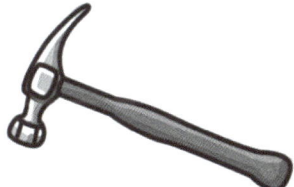

Metals and non-metals

Metal or non-metal?

1 Work with a partner. Look at these pictures and then complete the table below.

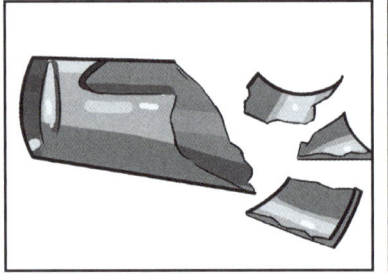
a

b

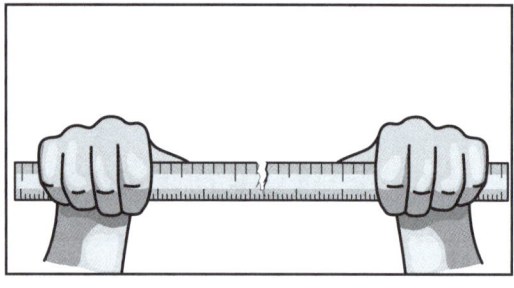
c

Which picture is it?

d

	Picture
1 A metal being bent	
2 A metal being hammered into shape	
3 A non-metal that has broken	
4 A non-metal snapping	

2 Find some objects in the room made of non-metals.

Draw two of your objects.

Properties of metals and non-metals

1. Look at these objects. Think about the materials they are made of.

   Circle all the non-metals.

2. Write one property of each of these materials.

   You can use the words in the box below to help you. Use the words more than once.

   fabric: _____

   paper: _____

   plastic: _____

   pottery: _____

   wood: _____

   | dull   hard   see-through   shiny   soft   stretchy   waterproof |

2 What is it Made of?

Useful materials

Making a model bridge and testing it

 Look at the bridges below.

Which bridge is the strongest? _____

How do you know? _____

Now make some bridges that you can test.

Use cardboard. Try different shapes.

Draw the strongest bridge you made.

More useful metal objects

1 Look at the photographs of metal objects. Draw a line to match each object with its name.

2 Circle the names of two objects that are sometimes made from gold.

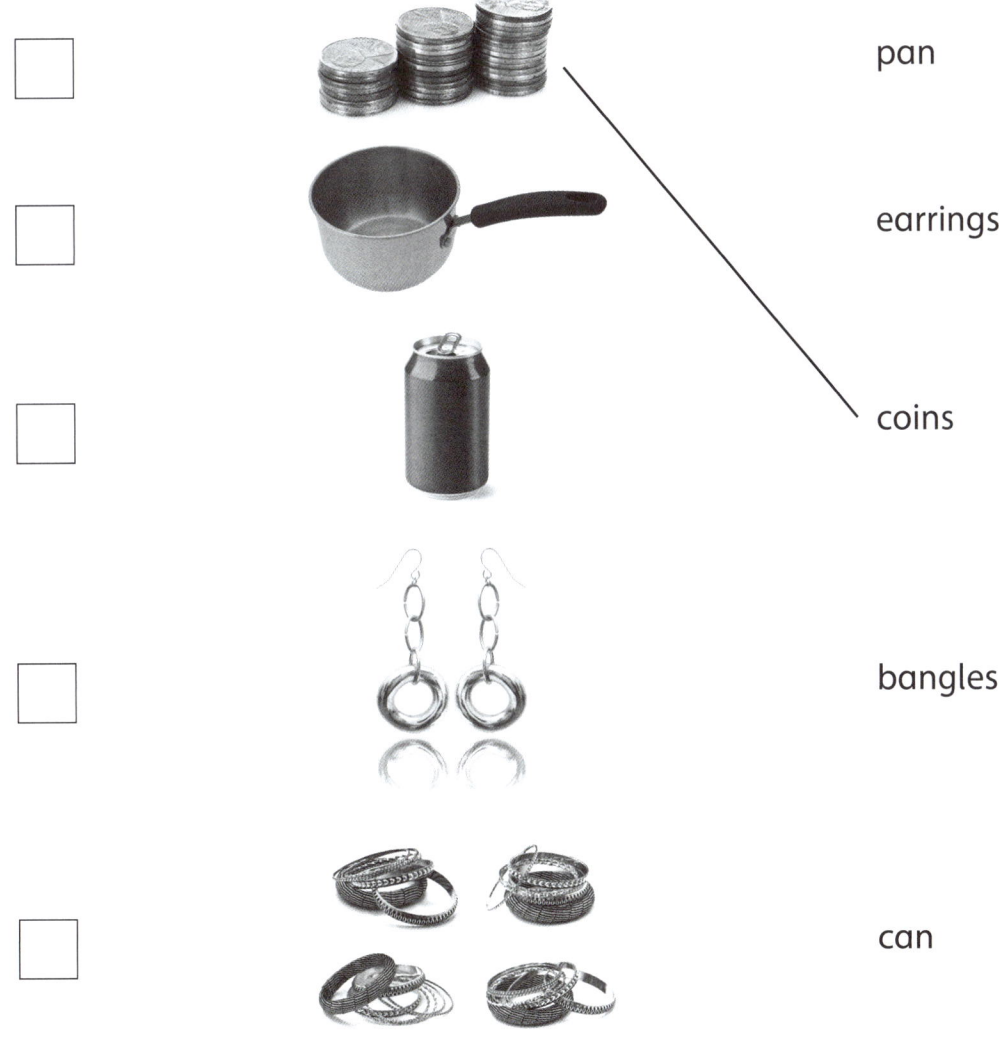

pan

earrings

coins

bangles

can

3 Tick ✓ the objects you have seen.

Stretch zone

Choose one object and tell someone why it is useful.

Sorting materials into groups

Soft or hard?

 1 Join the dots to write the words.

2 Sort different objects into hoops on the floor. Place each object in the correct sorting circle.

Then write the name of each item in the correct sorting circle below.

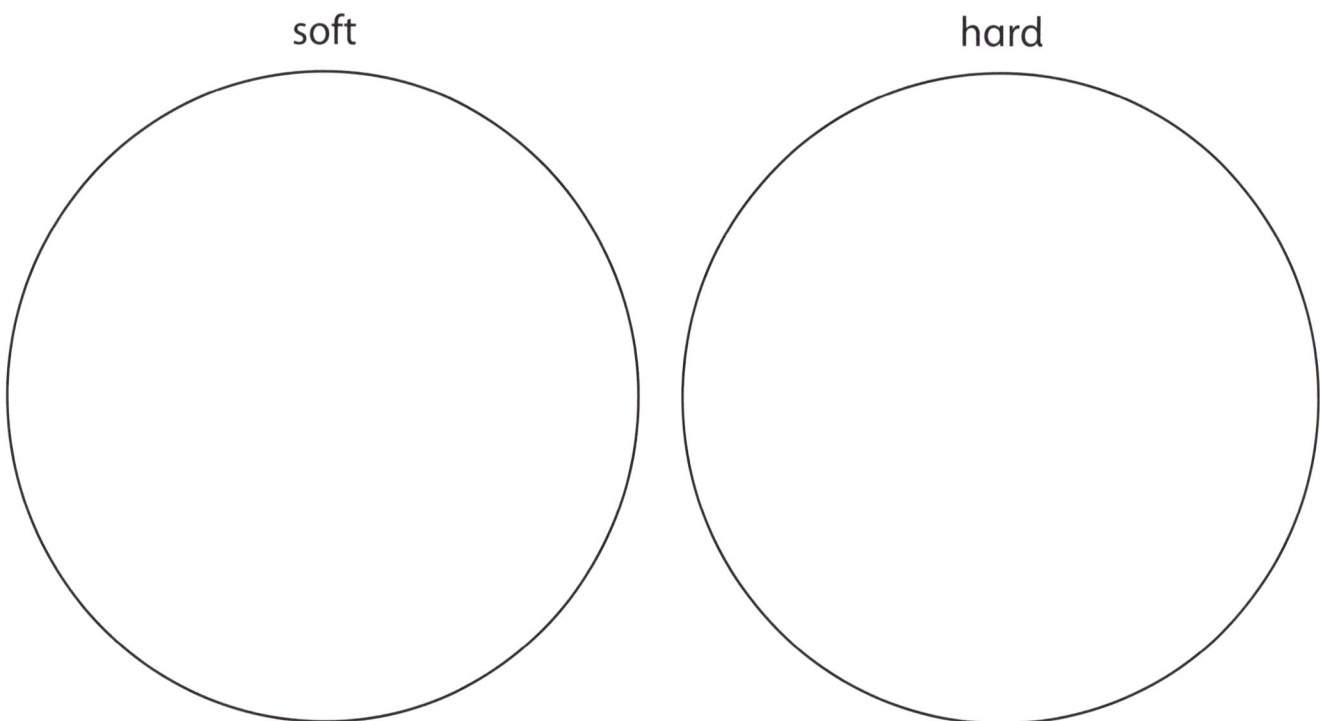

Making music

Stretch zone

Metals make a sound when you tap them.

If you hit a metal dish or pan with a pencil, it makes a sound.

Try it.

1. Your teacher will give you some objects.

    Gently, tap each object with a pencil.

    Does it make a sound like a metal?

2. Sort all of the objects into metals and non-metals.

3. Make up a tune tapping the metal objects.

    Did everyone like the music being made? Think about the reasons for this.

What I have learned about materials

1. Think about what you have learned.
2. Talk to a friend about something that went well in this unit.
3. Tick ✓ the boxes to rate yourself.

I can use my senses to explore different materials.	That's easy. ☐ That's challenging. ☐	Pages 34–35
I know that materials have properties, including being waterproof, stretchy and being able to float or sink.	That's easy. ☐ That's challenging. ☐	Pages 36–41
I know that metals are useful materials.	That's easy. ☐ That's challenging. ☐	Pages 42–43
I know that materials are either metals or non-metals.	That's easy. ☐ That's challenging. ☐	Pages 44–45
I can name some common materials.	That's easy. ☐ That's challenging. ☐	Pages 46–47
I can sort materials into groups based on their properties.	That's easy. ☐ That's challenging. ☐	Pages 48–49

☺ If you want to know more or need to check, go back to the pages in your Student Book.

Investigate like a scientist

Testing designs

1 **Designing and testing a model bridge**

You will make a spaghetti bridge.

a Use dry spaghetti and sticky tape to make a spaghetti bridge.

 The bridge has to cross a gap of 50 centimetres.

b Design and build your bridge.

2 **Which bag is stronger?**

You will find out which of three bags is stronger.

a Collect three different plastic bags.

b Plan how you will test to see which can hold the most weight before breaking.

c Carry out your test.

d Record your results.

Warning! Make sure none of the weights can fall and hurt you.

3 Pushes and Pulls

Key words

1. Push your seat under the desk.

   Pull your chair from under the desk.

   This will help you decide if there is a push or a pull **force**.

When you **push** an object, it moves **away** from you.

When you **pull** an object, it moves **towards** you.

2. Join the dots to find the forces for each picture.

   a

   b

push

pull

Introduction

Pushes and pulls

Pushes and pulls are forces that make things move.

1   Your teacher will give you a beanbag.

Sit across the desk from a partner.

Push the beanbag across the desk and say out loud 'push'.

Pull the beanbag across the desk and say out loud 'pull'.

Warning! Do not throw the bean bag as it could hurt someone.

2   Look around the room.

Where are pushes used? Where are pulls used?

Draw a push being used.   Draw a pull being used.

Stopping and starting

Using your body

1 What happens to your arms as you walk?

 Walk to the other side of the room.

   a Talk about how your arms moved.

      Walk back across the room.

   b When you stopped walking, how did your arms move?

   c Complete these sentences. Use the words in the box to help you.

      When I walked quickly, my arms _____.

      When I walked slowly, my arms _____.

      When I stopped walking, my arms _____.

| moved quickly | moved slowly | stopped moving |

2 Play a stopping and starting game.

   Use your feet to move a ball around.

   a Can you slow the ball down or speed it up? How did you do this?

   b How will you stop the ball?

Talk about your answers. Can you use the words 'push' and 'pull' to say how you moved the ball?

Toy car

How can you stop a moving toy car?

 a Talk about all the different ways you can stop a moving toy car.

b Write all the ways you have talked about.

_____
_____
_____
_____

c Predict which will be the best way to stop the toy car.

_____
_____

d Try all the ways you talked about. Was your prediction correct? Circle your answer.

yes   **no**

 Stretch zone

Share your investigation results with other groups. Compare your findings.

Did all the groups stop their cars in the same way? Circle your answer.

yes   **no**

Look at things moving in wind

Looking at flags

1. Talk about when you have seen flags moving.

   a Can you see any moving flags around you?

   yes   **no**

   b What makes flags move?

   c Draw what the flags will look like if the force of the wind stops.

2. How many things have you seen moving in the wind? Write some examples in the table. One has been done for you.

Example	Where I saw it
Clothes drying	In a garden

Making bunting

1. Bunting is a party decoration. You will make a long string of bunting.

   a Your teacher will give you a triangle cut out of card with two holes at the top edge.

   b Use paint or pens to create your own design, or use the triangle to cut out bunting from fabric.

   c Your teacher will help you join your bunting pieces together with string or ribbon.

2. Choose a good place to hang your bunting.

   a How will you make sure it blows in the wind?

   b How will you attach each end of your bunting?

3. Watch your bunting.

   a Is it blowing in the wind?

   b Should you move it to a better place?

Look at things moving in water and wind

Making a sailing boat

 This activity supports the investigation on page 58 of your Student Book.

Work with a partner for this activity.

You will need: a plastic bottle top, a triangle of paper, some modelling clay, and a piece of straw.

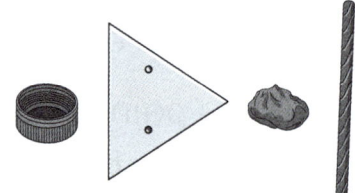

1 a Put the modelling clay in the bottle top.

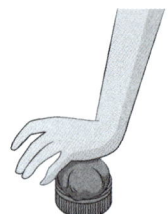

b There will be two holes in the piece of paper.

Push the straw through the holes.

c Push the straw into the modelling clay.

You have made a sailing boat!

d Sail your boat in a water trough or container.

2 Circle the answers to these questions about your boat.

a Does it float?   **yes**   **no**

b Carefully use your hand to move the water behind your boat.

Does this make it move?   **yes**   **no**

c Try to make the boat move from side to side.

Be careful not to sink your boat.

Making boats move

1 You will use a small boat and a kitchen baster.

   a Fill the baster with air.

      Hold it behind the boat and squeeze out the air.

   b Practise this for a few minutes. Can you make the boat go faster?

2 What makes your boat move faster?

   Tick ✓ the correct answer.

   Blowing the air from the baster onto the bottle top.   ☐

   Blowing air from the baster onto the sail.   ☐

3 What will happen if you use water in the baster?

   a Circle your prediction.

      yes, it would move   **no, it would not move**

   b Test your prediction.

      Circle your result.

      yes, it did move   **no, it did not move**

Explore how things move (pushes and pulls)

More pushes and pulls

  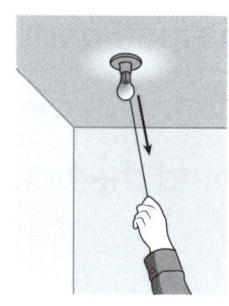 

1 Fill in the missing words. Use these words: push   pull

The toy moves when we _____ it.

The pushchair moves when we _____ it.

The light switch cord moves when we _____ it.

The bricks fall over when we _____ them.

2 Find some examples of pushes and pulls around the room.

Take a photograph or draw a picture of a pull or a push you have seen today.

A pull I have seen and used	**A push I have seen and used**

Examples of pushing and pulling

 1 Look at this picture and talk about what the person is doing.

Sometimes you have to pull something very strongly!

 2 Talk about when you have pulled something strongly or seen others do this. Draw a picture of this in the space below.

3 A time when I pushed something strongly was _____
_____.

 **Stretch zone**

Imagine there are no push or pull forces. Which games would not work?

Fast and slow-moving objects

Fast and slow

1 Can you say this word very slowly? Can you make it last for ten seconds?

Faster

Now can you say it faster and faster? Can you say it ten times in ten seconds?

2 Can you say this word very quickly? Can you say it ten times in ten seconds?

Slower

Say it slower and slower. Can you make it last for ten seconds?

3 Look at the pictures.

Think about how the objects and people are moving. Choose whether they are moving fast, are moving slowly, or have stopped.

Write the correct answer below each picture.

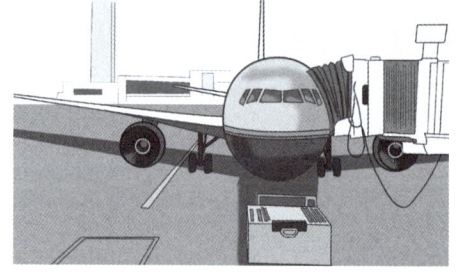

Swing

1 Talk about the picture with your partner. How could you help the child to swing faster?

2 Read out the sentences and words to each other. Circle the correct words.

If the mother pushes the swing harder, it will	move slower	move faster	stop
If the mother stops pushing the swing, it will	move slower	move faster	stop
If the mother pushes the swing more gently, it will	move slower	move faster	stop

3 Can you think of some examples of things that move slowly and things that move fast?

Choose five objects that can move fast. Choose five objects that can move slowly. Write them in the table.

Fast object	Slow object

Exploring the movement of toys

Making a toy car move

This activity supports the investigation on page 64 of your Student Book.

1 How do you think a toy car moves?

Talk about your ideas with a partner. Now try to move a toy car. Answer the questions.

  a How did you start the car moving?

  _____

  b What happened to the car when you pulled it towards you?

  _____

  c What did the car do when you did not touch it?

  _____

2 Find places in school where things are moving.

Write what you see. Find six examples.

Object moving	Describe the movement

Design and build a moving vehicle

> **Stretch zone**
>
> Can you design and build a moving boat, car or aeroplane?
> Your teacher will give you some materials to use.

I am going to make a _____
_____.

a What will you use to make the vehicle? Remember it must move.

_____
_____

b What force will make it move? Choose from push, pull, wind or water.

_____

c Have a race. Whose boat/car/aeroplane was faster? What made it go fast?

_____
_____

What I have learned about pushes and pulls

1. Think about what you have learned.
2. Talk to a friend about something that went well in this unit.
3. Tick ✓ the boxes to rate yourself.

I know that forces make things stop and start.	That's easy. ☐ That's challenging. ☐	Pages 54–55
I know that things can move fast and slowly, and in different directions.	That's easy. ☐ That's challenging. ☐	Pages 56–57
I know that wind and water can make things move.	That's easy. ☐ That's challenging. ☐	Pages 58–59
I know that pushes and pulls are forces that make things move.	That's easy. ☐ That's challenging. ☐	Pages 60–61
I understand how forces make things go faster and slower.	That's easy. ☐ That's challenging. ☐	Pages 62–63
I know that when something moves, a push or a pull must have made it move.	That's easy. ☐ That's challenging. ☐	Pages 64–65

If you want to know more or need to check, go back to the pages in your Student Book.

 **Investigate like a scientist**

Playing with pushes and pulls

Work with a partner. You will need a soft ball.

You will use some pieces of paper with these words on them:

| faster | pull | push | slower |

1. **Put the pieces of paper in a pile, face down.**
2. **Take turns to pick a word and read it out loud.**
3. **Place the words on the desk in the order you picked them.**
4. **Take turns to follow the instructions, using the ball.**

 Did you follow the instructions? Was this easy or difficult? How did you slow the ball down or speed it up?

4 Making Sounds

Key words

We hear sounds.

1 Practise saying 'sound'.
2 In the space below, draw pictures of all the sounds you can hear.

   Are they loud or quiet sounds?

   Can you hear any voices?

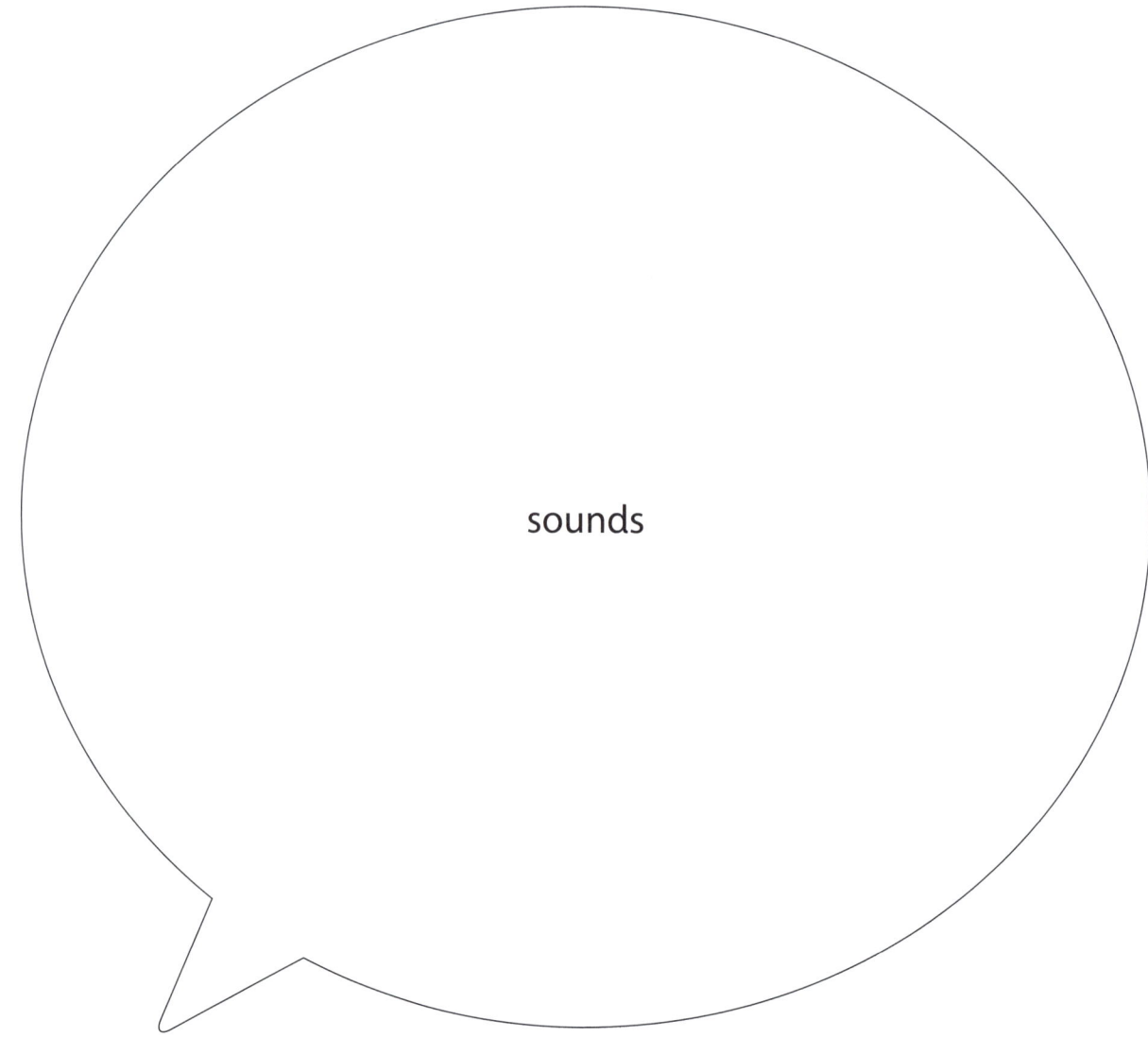

sounds

Introduction

Making more music

Sometimes we make a sound just because we like it.

Music can make people happy.

1 a List all the musical instruments that you know.

_____

_____

_____

_____

_____

b How many musical instruments are on your list? _____

2 Draw one musical instrument that you have played.

Talking and listening

Your voice

1 Join the dots to write the words.

2 How many different sounds can you make with your voice?

Write four sounds in the table. An example has been done for you.

Student	Sound 1	Sound 2	Sound 3	Sound 4	Sound 5
You	whisper				

3 Choose one of your sounds. Was your sound loud or quiet? Tick ✓ the answer.

loud ☐   quiet ☐

Sing!

You are going to sing some musical notes.

You will need: a stopwatch or a clock with a second hand.

1 One person sings a musical note, 'la'.
2 The next person must sing exactly the same note. Take it in turns to sing the note.
3 Now take it in turns to sing the note for as long as possible.
4 How long can each person sing the note? Fill in the table.

Name of person	Time in seconds

5 Now use different musical notes. Can you make it sound like music?

Making sounds

Clap your hands

This activity supports the investigation on page 72 of your Student Book.

1 Work with a partner. How can you clap quietly and loudly?

   a Clap your hands together and say the word 'clap'.

   b Now listen to your partner clapping their hands.

      Clap your hands hard.

      Clap your hands gently.

2 Complete the sentences. Draw a circle around the best answer.

When I clap my hands together hard, the sound is   **louder quieter**.

When I clap my hands together gently, the sound is   **louder quieter**.

3 Think of one of your favourite songs.

Clap your hands in time to the song. Do not sing the song.

Ask your partner to guess the song.

Make music using your lips

You are going to make a kazoo.

You will need: a comb and a thin piece of paper or tracing paper.

1. Fold the paper around the comb.

2. Hold your kazoo to your lips with your mouth closed.

Make sure your lips are dry.

Then hum a tune onto the paper.

3. Perform a tune.

Did other people recognise the tune?

Quiet and loud sounds

Listen carefully

This activity supports the investigation on page 74 of your Student Book.

1 Sit quietly.
2 Listen carefully.
3 Write three sounds you can hear.

Are the sounds loud or quiet? Circle the answer.

Sound 1 _____ **loud   quiet**

Sound 2 _____ **loud   quiet**

Sound 3 _____ **loud   quiet**

4 Choose one of the sounds. What made the sound?

Draw a picture of what made the sound.

Measuring sounds in school

Stretch zone

This activity supports the investigation on page 75 of your Student Book.

You are going to go on a listening walk.

1 Predict where you will hear the loudest and quietest sounds:

   I predict that I will find the loudest sound in the _____.

   I predict that I will find the quietest sound in the _____.

2 Go on a listening walk. Complete the table of results.

Sound	Where you heard it	Is the sound loud or quiet, or both?
Telephone ringing	In the hallway	loud

3 Look at the table of results.

   Where did you hear the loudest sound? _____

   Where did you hear the quietest sound? _____

4 Making Sounds

Sounds and moving about

Sounds near and far

It is useful to know whether sounds are near to us or far away.

You are going to explore some near and far sounds.

1 Listen carefully. Colour in the box below if you can hear the sound.

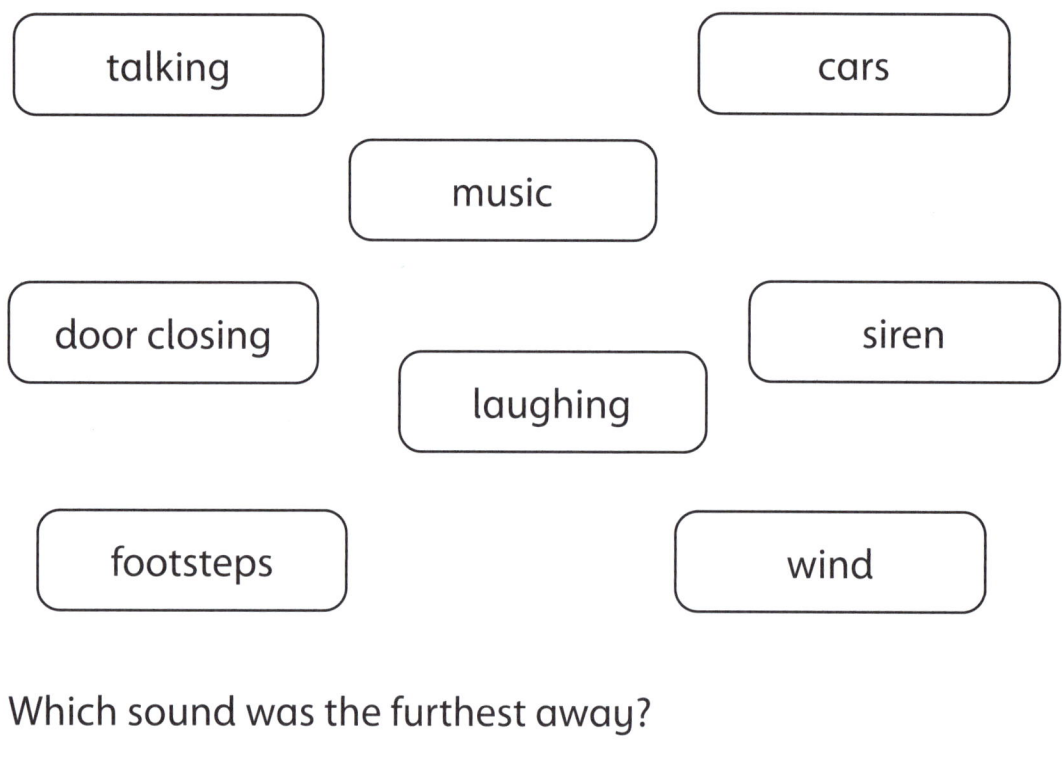

Which sound was the furthest away?

_____

2 Find out what happens to sounds when we get further away from them.

One of you is the 'Listener'. Move away from the Listener slowly as you speak your name.

Measure how far away you are when the Listener can no longer hear you.

Surprise!

Play a game. You need to try to be as quiet as possible.

a One person stands at the front of the room. They must face the wall so they cannot see the others in the room.

b Everyone else stands at the back of the room.

c The person at the front of the room says 'start'.

d Everyone must move towards the person at the front. They must move as slowly and quietly as they can.

e If the person at the front hears a sound, they turn around quickly. Anyone they see moving goes back to the beginning.

Who can reach the person at the front without being heard?

Sounds around us

Moving quietly

This activity supports the investigation on page 78 of your Student Book.

1 How does the leopard's feet help it to move quietly? _____

2 You are going to design and make some special shoes to help you move quietly.

> **You could use:** paper, card, sponge, cloth (such as an old towel). You will also need sticky tape and string or elastic bands. Ask an adult before you use anything.

a Choose the best material, then make your very quiet shoes. Fix the shoes to your feet with string or elastic bands.

b The main material I used was _____.

c Now try to walk up behind someone very quietly so that they do not hear you.

Did you reach the person before they heard you?

Circle your answer.   **yes**   **no**

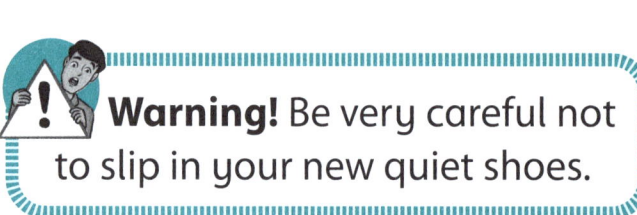

Warning! Be very careful not to slip in your new quiet shoes.

Useful loud noises

These emergency vehicles may not look like the ones you have seen. Different countries have different types of emergency vehicles.

1 Think about all the emergency vehicles you have seen.

   Draw a picture of one emergency vehicle.

2 All emergency vehicles have sirens.

   Try to make the noise of the siren on your emergency vehicle.

3 Why do vehicles have sirens? Use the words in the box below in your answer.

   | busy roads   danger   drivers   emergency   help   speed |

How we hear sounds

Hearing

This activity supports the investigation on page 80 of your Student Book.

1 Complete the sentence using the correct word in the box.

> ear   eye   hand   head

I use my _____s to hear.

2 Do you think you can hear with only one ear?

   a Sit in a safe place. Listen carefully to the sounds around you.
      Write four sounds you hear.

   ☐ 1 _____   ☐ 2 _____

   ☐ 3 _____   ☐ 4 _____

   b Close your eyes and listen carefully. Tick ✓ the sounds you can still hear.

   c Open your eyes, cover your left ear with your hand, and listen. Circle the sounds you can still hear.

   d Now cover just your right ear and listen. Underline the sounds you can still hear.

3 Did you hear better with your eyes open or closed?

   eyes open ☐   eyes closed ☐

4 Did you hear better with one ear or with two ears?

   one ear ☐   two ears ☐

Measuring sounds in decibels

Sound is measured in decibels.

A loud sound has many decibels. A quiet sound has only a few decibels.

You can measure how loud or quiet a sound is by using a sound-level meter.

Look at the table of sound-level meter readings.

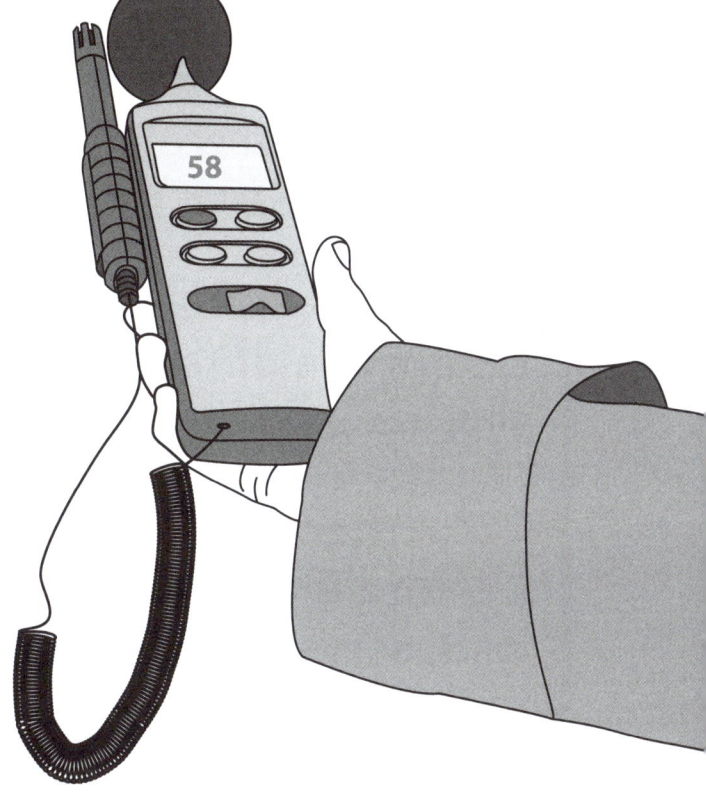

Sound	Decibels
Whispering	30
Road drill	95
Lawn mower	107
Live music	115
Talking	60
Jet engine	140
Train whistle	90

1. Which is the loudest sound? Colour the box that shows the decibels. Use red.

2. Which is the quietest sound? Colour the box that shows the decibels. Use green.

3. Sounds that are 95 decibels or louder can damage our hearing. Put a cross ✗ next to all the sounds that can damage our hearing.

What I have learned about making sounds

1 Think about what you have learned.
2 Talk to a friend about something that went well in this unit.
3 Tick ✓ the boxes to rate yourself.

I know that there are many things that make sounds.	That's easy. ☐ That's challenging. ☐	Pages 70–71
I can make different sounds with my voice and my body.	That's easy. ☐ That's challenging. ☐	Pages 72–73
I know that some sounds are loud, some sounds are quiet and some sounds are both loud and quiet.	That's easy. ☐ That's challenging. ☐	Pages 74–75
I know that when sounds move away from us they get quieter.	That's easy. ☐ That's challenging. ☐	Pages 76–79
I know that we use both of our ears together to help us hear better.	That's easy. ☐ That's challenging. ☐	Pages 80–81

☺ If you want to know more or need to check, go back to the pages in your Student Book.

Investigate like a scientist

Comparing different sounds

1 **You are going to work like a scientist and investigate sound.**

   Your teacher will tell you where to stand.

   a Close your eyes.

   b Walk forward with your eyes closed.

   c Your teacher will make a sound.

   d Put your hand up when you can no longer hear the sound.

   e Open your eyes and put a sticky label where you are standing.

   f Go back to the starting point and repeat this activity with different sounds.

2 **Are all your sticky labels in the same place?**

   _____

3 **Can you hear all of the sounds the same? Explain the differences.**

   _____
   _____
   _____
   _____

5 Plants and the Seasons

Key words

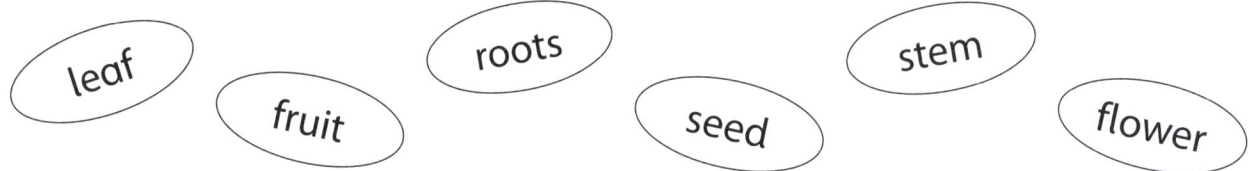

1 Find two key words beginning with the letter f.

   Say these words out loud.

2 Now find any objects in the picture that match these two key words.

   a Colour the objects in.

   b Tell your partner how many objects you found.

3 Look back at the key words at the top of the page.

   a Say the other key words out loud to your partner.

   b Can you find any objects in the picture that match these words? Tell your partner.

Introduction

Weather words

1 Follow the dots to write some of the key words for this unit.

season

rain

wind

2 Look at the pictures. Complete the following sentences.

a The weather in this picture is _____.

b The weather in this picture is _____.

Parts of a plant

Colour the parts of a plant

Colour the parts of a plant.
- a Colour the flower yellow.
- b Colour the leaves dark green.
- c Colour the stem light green.
- d Colour the roots brown.

Make a plant display

You are going to make a picture display of plants.

You can draw any plants you see at home, in a garden or in another place on your way to school.

You can also collect pictures from magazines or the internet.

These will help to make a colourful display.

Show as many different plants as you can. Label some examples of:

- leaves
- stems
- flowers
- roots.

Also label any plants we use for food.

Plant art gallery

Your teacher will put your display in a plant art gallery.

Look at all the other students' displays. Choose two ideas you want to use in future. It is good to learn from each other.

Looking at wild and garden plants

Is it a tree or a shrub?

a Which is a shrub and which is a tree?

Draw a line to link the plant with its name. One has been done for you.

b Tell your partner how you knew the difference between a tree and a shrub.

Survey of flowering plants

Go outdoors. Look for trees and shrubs.

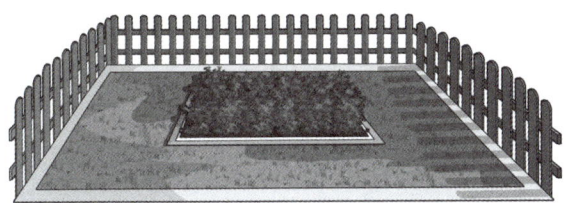 

1 Draw one tree that you found. Find out its name.

_____

2 Draw one shrub that you found. Find out its name.

_____

Weather

Predicting the weather

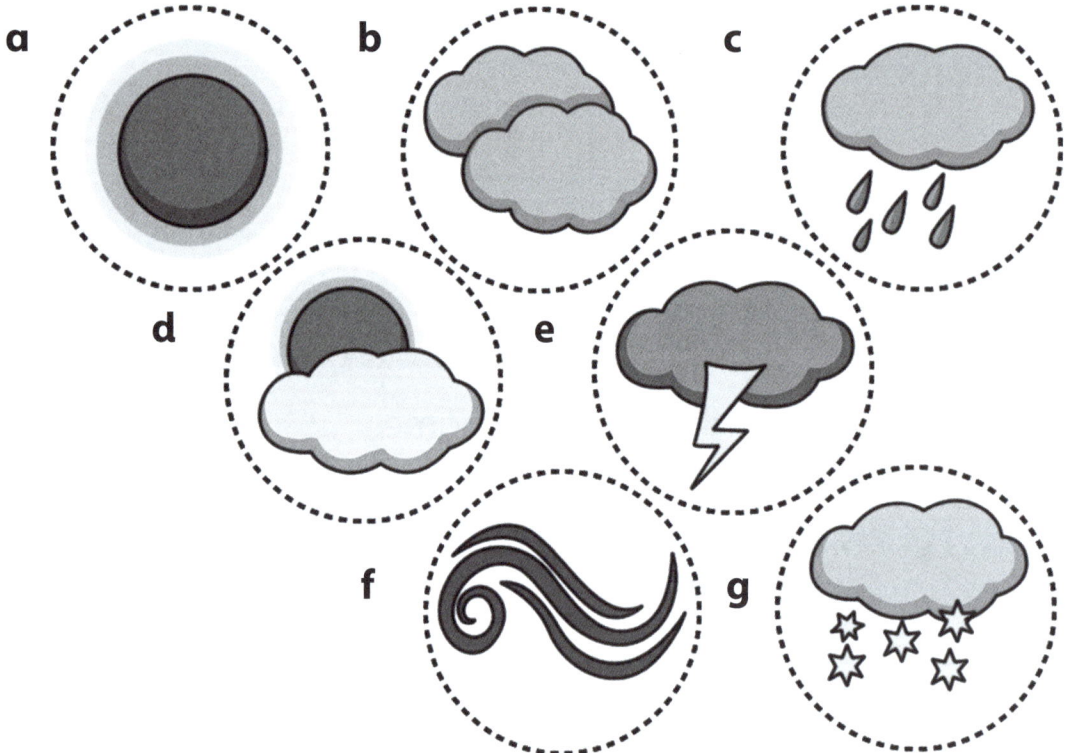

 **1** Talk about the weather symbols.

Which picture shows a sunny day? _____

Which picture shows a windy day? _____

Which picture shows a rainy day? _____

2 Observe the weather for five days. Write the letter of the weather symbol in the table.

	Day 1	Day 2	Day 3	Day 4	Day 5	Prediction for day 6	Day 6
Weather symbol							

3 Was your prediction for day 6 correct? Circle your answer.

yes   **no**

Types of weather

Look at the pictures.

a Think about why these people need to know what the weather will be like.

Think of a reason for each one. Tell your partner about your ideas.

b When may you next need to know the weather forecast?

_____

_____

The seasons

Which season is it?

autumn   spring   summer   winter

1. The seasons have been mixed up in the pictures.

   Draw a line to link each picture to its season. One has been done for you.

 2. Discuss the questions with a partner.

   a. Which seasons do you have in your area?

   b. How are plants different in the different seasons?

   c. How are animals different in the different seasons?

   d. What is your favourite season? Why?

Investigating seasons

This activity supports the investigation on page 93 of your Student Book.

1 Look around the playground or fields.

   Is it a warm or a cool time of year?

   Circle your answer. **warm** **cool**

2 Look at the plants you find. Circle your answers.

   Are they starting to grow? **yes** **no**

   Are any losing their leaves? **yes** **no**

3 Look at the animals. Circle your answers.

   Are there many? **yes** **no**

   Can you see young animals or eggs? **yes** **no**

4 Draw a picture of your area during spring.

Recording rainfall

Observing the weather

 1 Follow the dots to write the key word for this topic.

weather

2 Find out the meaning of this word.

Use a dictionary or ask someone if they know it.

Write the definition here.

_____

_____

_____

3 Look out of the window and answer the following question.

What is the weather like today?

Describe the weather. The words in the box below may help you.

_____

_____

_____

_____

calm	clear	cloudy	cold	dry	hot
	stormy	sunny	wet	windy	

Measuring rainfall

Use your rain gauge to measure rainfall.

Remember: Place some pebbles in the bottle and add water until they are covered.

Choose where to place your rain gauge.

Check it every day.

Write down how much rain you have collected.

Day	Amount of rainfall (in millimetres)

Which day had the most rain? _____

Which day had the least rain? _____

Observing and measuring the wind

Windsocks

We use windsocks to find out how windy it is. They also tell us the wind direction.

1 Make your own windsock.

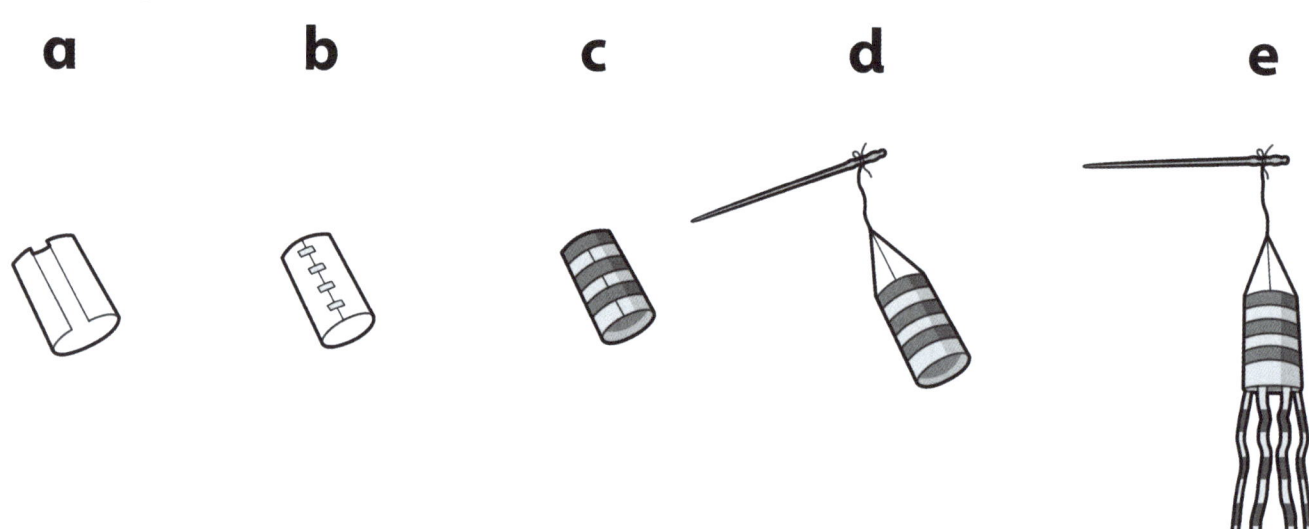

- a Roll some card so you make a tube.
- b Fix it together using tape or staples.
- c Colour your tube to make it bright.
- d Tie some string to the end of your tube.
- e Stick coloured paper or tissue to your tube. Make some long tails.
- f Hang your windsock outside.

2 What happens on windy days?

Wind speeds

Beaufort number	Wind speed (kph)		Effects on land
0	Under 2		Calm, smoke rises vertically
2	6–11		Wind felt on face, leaves rustle, wind vanes begin to move
4	20–28		Dust, leaves and loose paper blow about, small branches move
6	39–49		Large tree branches move
8	62–74		Twigs and small branches break off trees
10	89–102		Trees break and many buildings are damaged
12	118 or higher		Buildings are destroyed and large trees blow over

What would you see if the wind was 3 on the Beaufort scale?

What I have learned about plants and the seasons

 1 Think about what you have learned.
2 Talk to a friend about something that went well in this unit.
3 Tick ✓ the boxes to rate yourself.

I know the names of the main parts of a plant.	That's easy. ☐ That's challenging. ☐	Pages 86–87
I know the differences between wild and garden plants.	That's easy. ☐ That's challenging. ☐	Pages 88–89
I can identify the types of weather.	That's easy. ☐ That's challenging. ☐	Pages 90–91
I know about the different seasons.	That's easy. ☐ That's challenging. ☐	Pages 92–93
I can record rainfall and measure wind speeds.	That's easy. ☐ That's challenging. ☐	Pages 94–97

😊 If you want to know more or need to check, go back to the pages in your Student Book.

Investigate like a scientist

Making a model plant

You will work in a group to make a model plant.

1. Take the materials to your table.
2. Plan your model. Draw your model before you start to make it.

3. Work together to make the model.
4. Display your model. Make label cards to show each part of the plant.
5. Think of two ways that you could make your model better.

Quiz Yourself

How to use these questions

These quiz questions and activities are intended to encourage students to reflect on their learning and to reinforce their developing knowledge about scientific concepts in a fun way. They are flexible enough to be individual, pair or group activities. The questions can be used in a number of ways:

- Questions can be selected from this section to supplement work carried out during each module, to act as extra tasks and support for individuals, groups and whole classes. In this way, they can aid differentiation.
- Students can tackle the relevant questions at the end of each module to review learning and supplement the 'What I have learned' sections.
- Students can undertake questions at the end of a series of modules or even at the end of the year to review learning. The questions could be set in batches over a series of lessons or even taken as a small timed test – although this is not their main purpose.

① Exploring Animals

1. Are these animals vertebrates or invertebrates? Draw a line from each picture to the correct word. One has been done for you.

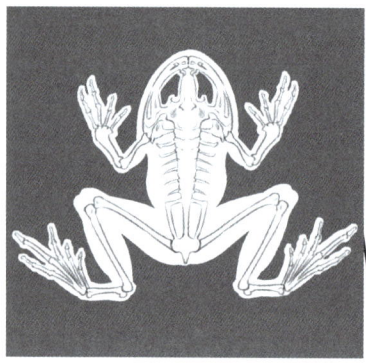

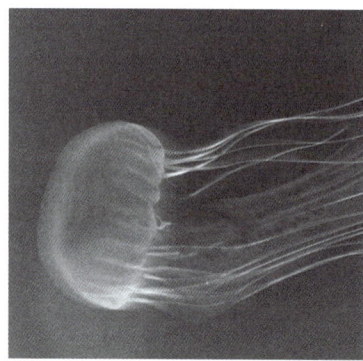
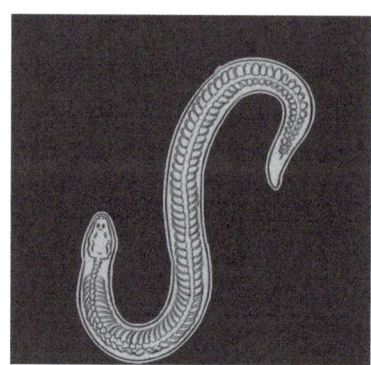

vertebrate   invertebrate

2. Look at the pictures. Which group does each animal belong to? Draw a line from each animal to the correct circle.

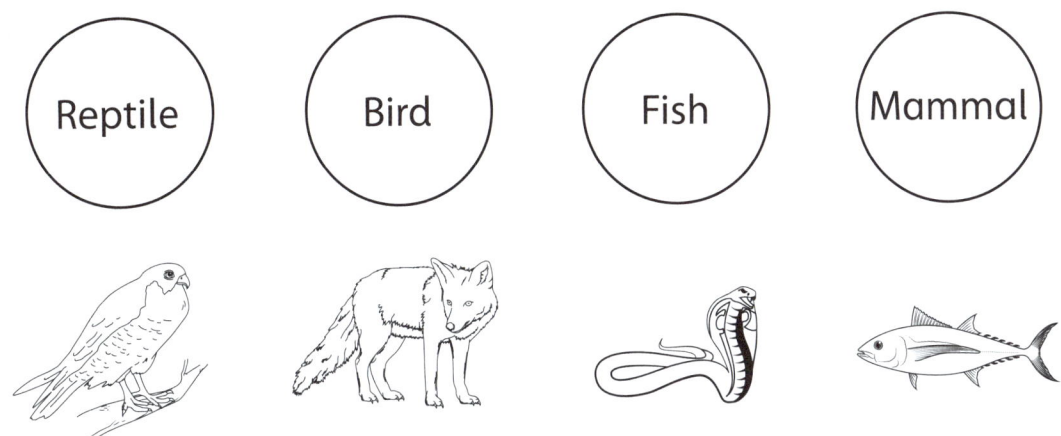

3. Colour the herbivore green. Colour the carnivore red. Colour the omnivore blue.

4 Draw a line from each part of the face to the correct sense.

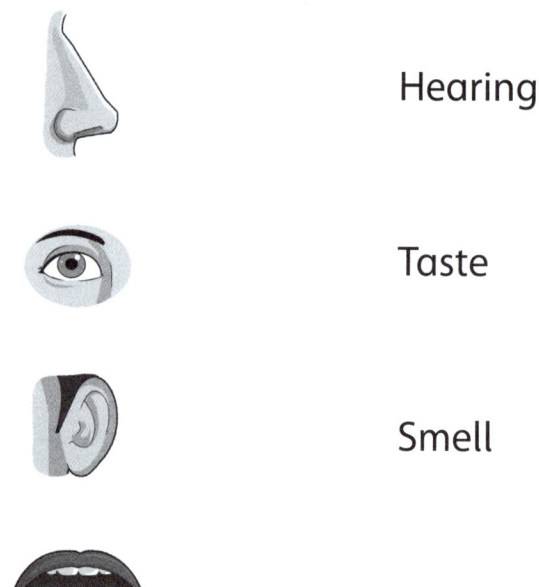

Hearing

Taste

Smell

Sight

5 Look at the picture. Label the child's head, arms, legs, hands and feet.

2 What is it Made of?

6 Follow the curly lines to match each object with its property. Write the property in the box.

Hard

Soft

Shiny

Bendy

7 Tick ✓ the material that is waterproof.

paper towel ☐   cloth ☐   plastic bag ☐

8 Look at the picture of the objects in a bowl of water.

a Write the letter F inside two objects that float.

b Write the letter S inside two objects that do not float.

Complete the missing word: These two objects s _ _ _ .

3 Pushes and Pulls

9 Colour the pictures. Use red to show pulls. Use blue to show pushes.

4 Making Sounds

10 Can you put the sounds in the correct order?

5 Plants and the Seasons

11 Draw a line from each label to the correct part of the plant.

- stem
- roots
- leaf
- flower

12 Write two words that describe the weather in each photograph. Use the words in the box to help you.

| cloudy   cold   dry   hot   rainy   windy |

13 Draw a line from each season to the correct picture. One has been done for you.

summer   winter   spring   autumn